CW01304736

The Utimate Ninja Dual Zone Air Fryer Cookbook

1600 Days Recipes for Healthy and Delicious Meals
Mastering the Art of Dual Zone Air Frying

Jessie P. Clark

CONTENTS

INTRODUCTION **8**

Chapter 1 Basic Information **9**

Ninja Dual Zone Air Fryer 9

The Difference Between Air Frying and Deep Frying 9

Some Usage Tips and Precautions for the Dual Zone Air Fryer 10

Chapter 2 Breakfast Recipes **11**

Pumpkin French Toast Casserole With Sweet And Spicy Twisted Bacon 11

Buttermilk Biscuits With Roasted Stone Fruit Compote 12

Egg With Baby Spinach 13

Hash Browns 13

Quiche Breakfast Peppers 14

Bagels 14

Blueberry Coffee Cake And Maple Sausage Patties 15

Egg White Muffins 16

Easy Pancake Doughnuts 16

Air Fryer Sausage Patties 17

Banana Muffins 17

Pepper Egg Cups 18

Spinach And Red Pepper Egg Cups With Coffee-glazed Canadian Bacon 18

Bacon And Egg Omelet 19

Healthy Oatmeal Muffins 19

Lemon-cream Cheese Danishes Cherry Danishes 20

Breakfast Stuffed Peppers 20

Honey Banana Oatmeal 21

Sweet Potato Hash 21

Spinach Egg Muffins 22

Strawberry Baked Oats Chocolate Peanut Butter Baked Oats 22

Sausage & Butternut Squash 23

Breakfast Cheese Sandwich 23

Roasted Oranges 24

Sausage Hash And Baked Eggs 24

Chapter 3 Snacks And Appetizers Recipes **25**

Cheese Stuffed Mushrooms 25

Crispy Chickpeas 25

Parmesan Crush Chicken 26

Zucchini Chips 26
Potato Tater Tots 27
Sweet Bites 27
Crab Cake Poppers 28
Fried Pickles 28
Crispy Popcorn Shrimp 29
Cheese Corn Fritters 29
Ravioli 30
Beef Jerky Pineapple Jerky 30
Chili-lime Crispy Chickpeas Pizza-seasoned Crispy Chickpeas 31
Onion Rings 32
Jalapeño Popper Chicken 32
Chicken Crescent Wraps 33
Chicken Stuffed Mushrooms 33
Buffalo Wings Honey-garlic Wings 34
Tater Tots 34
Mac And Cheese Balls 35
Stuffed Mushrooms 35
Spicy Chicken Tenders 36
Healthy Chickpea Fritters 36
Healthy Spinach Balls 37
Tasty Sweet Potato Wedges 37

Chapter 4 Beef, Pork, And Lamb Recipes 38

Pork Chops And Potatoes 38
Gochujang Brisket 38
Yogurt Lamb Chops 39
Tomahawk Steak 39
Steak Fajitas With Onions And Peppers 40
Short Ribs & Root Vegetables 40
Beef And Bean Taquitos With Mexican Rice 41
Steak Bites With Cowboy Butter 42
Pork Chops With Broccoli 42
Balsamic Steak Tips With Roasted Asparagus And Mushroom Medley 43
Tasty Pork Skewers 43
Jerk-rubbed Pork Loin With Carrots And Sage 44
Italian Sausages With Peppers, Potatoes, And Onions 44
Barbecue Ribs With Roasted Green Beans And Shallots 45
Beef & Broccoli 46
Lamb Chops With Dijon Garlic 46
Garlic-rosemary Pork Loin With Scalloped Potatoes And Cauliflower 47
Mongolian Beef With Sweet Chili Brussels Sprouts 48

Pork Katsu With Seasoned Rice 49
Steak And Mashed Creamy Potatoes 50
Air Fried Lamb Chops 50
Steak And Asparagus Bundles 51
Juicy Pork Chops 51
Air Fryer Meatloaves 52
Chipotle Beef 52

Chapter 5 Poultry Recipes 53
Chicken Parmesan With Roasted Lemon-parmesan Broccoli 53
Chicken Drumettes 54
Cornish Hen 54
Crispy Sesame Chicken 55
Air Fried Chicken Legs 55
Chicken And Potatoes 56
Chicken Caprese 56
Coconut Chicken Tenders With Broiled Utica Greens 57
Chicken Drumsticks 58
Chicken & Veggies 58
Spicy Chicken 59
Greek Chicken Meatballs 59
Bang-bang Chicken 60
Chicken Kebabs 60
Sweet-and-sour Chicken With Pineapple Cauliflower Rice 61
Brazilian Chicken Drumsticks 62
Buttermilk Fried Chicken 62
Air-fried Turkey Breast With Roasted Green Bean Casserole 63
Cornish Hen With Asparagus 64
Wings With Corn On The Cob 64
Balsamic Duck Breast 65
Juicy Duck Breast 65
Chili Chicken Wings 66
Chicken Parmesan 66
Chicken Fajitas With Street Corn 67

Chapter 6 Fish And Seafood Recipes 68
Tilapia With Mojo And Crispy Plantains 68
Herb Lemon Mussels 69
Blackened Mahimahi With Honey-roasted Carrots 69
Shrimp Po'boys With Sweet Potato Fries 70
Salmon Nuggets 71
Pretzel-crusted Catfish 71

Garlic Shrimp With Pasta Alfredo 72
Herb Tuna Patties 72
Shrimp With Lemon And Pepper 73
Salmon With Green Beans 73
Furikake Salmon 74
Roasted Salmon And Parmesan Asparagus 74
Glazed Scallops 75
Lemon Pepper Fish Fillets 75
Tuna Patties 76
Southwestern Fish Fillets 77
Healthy Lobster Cakes 77
Bang Bang Shrimp 78
Shrimp Skewers 78
Two-way Salmon 79
Smoked Salmon 79
Seafood Shrimp Omelet 80
Fish And Chips 80
Spicy Salmon Fillets 81
Air Fryer Calamari 81

Chapter 7 Vegetables And Sides Recipes 82

Delicious Potatoes & Carrots 82
Curly Fries 82
Jerk Tofu With Roasted Cabbage 83
Garlic-herb Fried Squash 84
Rosemary Asparagus & Potatoes 84
Cheesy Potatoes With Asparagus 85
Sweet Potatoes With Honey Butter 85
Green Beans With Baked Potatoes 86
Beets With Orange Gremolata And Goat's Cheese 86
Buffalo Seitan With Crispy Zucchini Noodles 87
Fried Avocado Tacos 88
Quinoa Patties 89
Veggie Burgers With "fried" Onion Rings 90
Acorn Squash Slices 91
Stuffed Sweet Potatoes 91
Air Fryer Vegetables 92
Balsamic Vegetables 92
Hasselback Potatoes 93
Bbq Corn 93
Balsamic-glazed Tofu With Roasted Butternut Squash 94
Fried Olives 94

Flavourful Mexican Cauliflower 95
Brussels Sprouts 95
Caprese Panini With Zucchini Chips 96
Air Fried Okra 97

Chapter 8 Desserts Recipes 98
Brownie Muffins 98
Lava Cake 98
Cinnamon Bread Twists 99
Honey Lime Pineapple 99
Cake In The Air Fryer 100
Bread Pudding 100
Air Fryer Sweet Twists 101
Delicious Apple Fritters 101
Air Fried Beignets 102
Apple Crisp 102
Lemony Sweet Twists 103
Baked Apples 103
Cinnamon Sugar Dessert Fries 104
Chocó Lava Cake 104
Walnut Baklava Bites Pistachio Baklava Bites 105
Strawberry Shortcake 105
Chocolate Cookies 106
Jelly Donuts 106
Chocolate Chip Muffins 107
Air Fried Bananas 107
Cinnamon-sugar "churros" With Caramel Sauce 108
Moist Chocolate Espresso Muffins 108
Strawberry Nutella Hand Pies 109
Chocolate Pudding 109
Fried Dough With Roasted Strawberries 110

INDEX 111

INTRODUCTION

Hi food lovers, thank you for purchasing my recipe book!

I'm Jessie, a home-based food writer writing about food, cooking, and food nutrition. I often share my thoughts on life, love and food on my blog, and I love food photography too. I grew up with a passion for cooking, first learning it from my grandfather, who was the head chef in the family. Influenced by him, I majored in food safety and health in college and now have a job I love.

In this book, we focus on sharing low-fat, low-oil air fryer recipes, many of which are also vegetarian-friendly. Whether you're a low-fat meat eater, flexitarian, vegetarian, vegan, or following a gluten-free and/or dairy-free diet, you're sure to find a recipe to suit your tastes.

Welcome to the exciting world of the Ninja Dual Zone Air Fryer! Say goodbye to traditional deep-frying and hello to delicious, crispy meals with significantly less oil and mess. This revolutionary kitchen appliance combines high-speed hot air circulation with two independent cooking zones, allowing you to cook two different dishes at once without any flavor mixing.

In this cookbook, you'll find a collection of mouth-watering recipes designed to make the most out of your Ninja Dual Zone Air Fryer. From juicy chicken wings and crispy french fries to delicate salmon and delectable desserts, you'll be amazed at how versatile and easy-to-use this appliance is.

But that's not all - we've also included helpful tips and tricks to help you get the most out of your air fryer, along with guidance on cooking times and temperatures for different types of food. Whether you're an experienced chef or a novice in the kitchen, the Ninja Dual Zone Air Fryer Cookbook has everything you need to create delicious and healthy meals for your family and friends.

So dust off your air fryer, grab your ingredients, and let's get cooking!

Chapter 1 Basic Information

Ninja Dual Zone Air Fryer

The air frying technology used in the Ninja Dual Zone Air Fryer offers a healthier cooking option because it uses hot air to circulate around the food, cooking it evenly and crisping it up without the need for large amounts of oil. This means that you can still enjoy the crispy texture and delicious taste of fried food without the added fat and calories. Additionally, the Ninja Dual Zone Air Fryer has a dual-zone cooking function, which allows you to cook two different foods at different temperatures and times, further enhancing its versatility and health benefits. With this technology, you can enjoy your favorite fried foods guilt-free and with less mess and cleanup.

The Difference Between Air Frying and Deep Frying

Air frying and deep frying are two different cooking methods with different outcomes. Air frying offers a healthier cooking option with less oil, lower calories, and faster cooking times than traditional deep frying.

Cooking oil: In deep frying, a large amount of oil is required to submerge the food completely, while in air frying, only a small amount of oil or no oil at all is required to cook the food.

Texture: Deep-fried foods tend to have a crispy, crunchy texture due to the high heat and oil used, while air-fried foods have a crispy exterior but a softer interior due to the circulating hot air.

Healthiness: Deep-fried foods are often high in calories and unhealthy fats, while air-fried foods are a healthier option as they use less oil and are lower in fat and calories.

Cooking time: Air frying is typically faster than deep frying, as the hot air circulates and cooks the food evenly from all sides, while in deep frying, the food needs to be submerged in oil and cooked for a longer period.

Some Usage Tips and Precautions for the Dual Zone Air Fryer

Read the user manual carefully before using the dual zone air fryer. It will give you important information about how to use the appliance safely and efficiently.

Always preheat the air fryer before cooking. This helps to ensure that your food is cooked evenly and thoroughly.

Make sure that the air fryer is placed on a level, stable surface before use.

Do not overfill the cooking baskets with food, as this can cause the air to circulate poorly and result in uneven cooking.

When cooking fatty foods, such as bacon or sausages, it is important to empty the drip tray regularly to avoid flare-ups or smoking.

Use the right cooking temperature and time for your food. You can consult the user manual or a cooking chart for guidance.

Always use oven mitts or gloves when handling the cooking baskets or trays, as they can become very hot during use.

Do not immerse the cooking baskets or trays in water. Instead, clean them with a soft sponge or cloth and soapy water.

When cleaning the dual zone air fryer, make sure it is unplugged and completely cooled down.

Chapter 2 Breakfast Recipes

Pumpkin French Toast Casserole With Sweet And Spicy Twisted Bacon

Servings:4

Cooking Time: 35 Minutes

Ingredients:

- FOR THE FRENCH TOAST CASSEROLE
- 3 large eggs
- 1 cup unsweetened almond milk
- 1 cup canned unsweetened pumpkin puree
- 2 teaspoons pumpkin pie spice
- ¼ cup packed light brown sugar
- 1 teaspoon vanilla extract
- 6 cups French bread cubes
- 1 teaspoon vegetable oil
- ¼ cup maple syrup
- FOR THE BACON
- 2 tablespoons light brown sugar
- ⅛ teaspoon cayenne pepper
- 8 slices bacon

Directions:

1. To prep the French toast casserole: In a shallow bowl, whisk together the eggs, almond milk, pumpkin puree, pumpkin pie spice, brown sugar, and vanilla.
2. Add the bread cubes to the egg mixture, making sure the bread is fully coated in the custard. Let sit for at least 10 minutes to allow the bread to soak up the custard.
3. To prep the bacon: In a small bowl, combine the brown sugar and cayenne.
4. Arrange the bacon on a cutting board in a single layer. Evenly sprinkle the strips with the brown sugar mixture. Fold the bacon strip in half lengthwise. Hold one end of the bacon steady and twist the other end so the bacon resembles a straw.
5. To cook the casserole and bacon: Brush the Zone 1 basket with the oil. Pour the French toast casserole into the Zone 1 basket, drizzle with maple syrup, and insert the basket in the unit. Install a crisper plate in the Zone 2 basket, add the bacon twists in a single layer, and insert the basket in the unit. For the best fit, arrange the bacon twists across the unit, front to back.
6. Select Zone 1, select BAKE, set the temperature to 330°F, and set the time to 35 minutes.
7. Select Zone 2, select AIR FRY, set the temperature to 400°F, and set the time to 12 minutes. Select SMART FINISH.
8. Press START/PAUSE to begin cooking.
9. When cooking is complete, transfer the bacon to a plate lined with paper towels. Let cool for 2 to 3 minutes before serving with the French toast casserole.

Nutrition Info:

- (Per serving) Calories: 601; Total fat: 28g; Saturated fat: 9g; Carbohydrates: 67g; Fiber: 2.5g; Protein: 17g; Sodium: 814mg

Buttermilk Biscuits With Roasted Stone Fruit Compote

Servings:4
Cooking Time: 20 Minutes

Ingredients:

- FOR THE BISCUITS
- 1⅓ cups all-purpose flour
- 2 teaspoons sugar
- 2 teaspoons baking powder
- ½ teaspoon baking soda
- ½ teaspoon kosher salt
- 4 tablespoons (½ stick) very cold unsalted butter
- ½ cup plus 1 tablespoon low-fat buttermilk
- FOR THE FRUIT COMPOTE
- 2 peaches, peeled and diced
- 2 plums, peeled and diced
- ¼ cup water
- 2 teaspoons honey
- ⅛ teaspoon ground ginger (optional)

Directions:

1. To prep the biscuits: In a small bowl, combine the flour, sugar, baking powder, baking soda, and salt. Using the large holes on a box grater, grate in the butter. Stir in the buttermilk to form a thick dough.
2. Place the dough on a lightly floured surface and gently pat it into a ½-inch-thick disc. Fold the dough in half, then rotate the whole thing 90 degrees, pat into a ½-inch thick disc and fold again. Repeat until you have folded the dough four times.
3. Pat the dough out a final time into a ½-inch-thick disc and use a 3-inch biscuit cutter to cut 4 biscuits from the dough (discard the scraps).
4. To prep the fruit compote: In a large bowl, stir together the peaches, plums, water, honey, and ginger (if using).
5. To cook the biscuits and compote: Install a crisper plate in the Zone 1 basket, place the biscuits in the basket, and insert the basket in the unit. Place the fruit in the Zone 2 basket and insert the basket in the unit.
6. Select Zone 1, select AIR FRY, set the temperature to 400°F, and set the time to 10 minutes.
7. Select Zone 2, select ROAST, set the temperature to 350°F, and set the time to 20 minutes. Select SMART FINISH.
8. Press START/PAUSE to begin cooking.
9. When the Zone 2 timer reads 10 minutes, press START/PAUSE. Remove the basket and stir the compote. Reinsert the basket and press START/PAUSE to resume cooking.
10. When cooking is complete, the biscuits will be golden brown and crisp on top and the fruit will be soft. Transfer the biscuits to a plate to cool. Lightly mash the fruit to form a thick, jammy sauce.
11. Split the biscuits in half horizontally and serve topped with fruit compote.

Nutrition Info:

- (Per serving) Calories: 332; Total fat: 12g; Saturated fat: 7.5g; Carbohydrates: 50g; Fiber: 2.5g; Protein: 6g; Sodium: 350mg

Egg With Baby Spinach

Servings:4
Cooking Time:12

Ingredients:

- Nonstick spray, for greasing ramekins
- 2 tablespoons olive oil
- 6 ounces baby spinach
- 2 garlic cloves, minced
- 1/3 teaspoon kosher salt
- 6-8 large eggs
- ½ cup half and half
- Salt and black pepper, to taste
- 8 Sourdough bread slices, toasted

Directions:

1. Grease 4 ramekins with oil spray and set aside for further use.
2. Take a skillet and heat oil in it.
3. Then cook spinach for 2 minutes and add garlic and salt black pepper.
4. Let it simmer for2more minutes.
5. Once the spinach is wilted, transfer it to a plate.
6. Whisk an egg into a small bowl.
7. Add in the spinach.
8. Whisk it well and then pour half and half.
9. Divide this mixture between 4 ramekins and remember not to overfill it to the top, leave a little space on top.
10. Put the ramekins in zone 1 and zone 2 baskets of the Ninja Foodie 2-Basket Air Fryer.
11. Press start and set zone 1 to AIR fry it at 350 degrees F for 8-12 minutes.
12. Press the MATCH button for zone 2.
13. Once it's cooked and eggs are done, serve with sourdough bread slices.

Nutrition Info:

- (Per serving) Calories 404| Fat 19.6g| Sodium 761mg | Carbs 40.1g | Fiber 2.5g| Sugar 2.5g | Protein 19.2g

Hash Browns

Servings: 4
Cooking Time: 5 Minutes

Ingredients:

- 4 frozen hash browns patties
- Cooking oil spray of choice

Directions:

1. Install a crisper plate in both drawers. Place half the hash browns in zone 1 and half in zone 2, then insert the drawers into the unit. Spray the hash browns with some cooking oil.
2. Select zone 1, select AIR FRY, set temperature to 390 degrees F/ 200 degrees C, and set time to 5 minutes.
3. Select MATCH to match zone 2 settings to zone 1. Press the START/STOP button to begin cooking.
4. When cooking is complete, remove the hash browns and serve.

Nutrition Info:

- (Per serving) Calories 130 | Fat 7g | Sodium 300mg | Carbs 15g | Fiber 2g | Sugar 0g | Protein 1g

Quiche Breakfast Peppers

Servings: 4
Cooking Time: 15 Minutes
Ingredients:

- 4 eggs
- ½ tsp garlic powder
- 112g mozzarella cheese, shredded
- 125g ricotta cheese
- 2 bell peppers, cut in half & remove seeds
- 7½g baby spinach, chopped
- 22g parmesan cheese, grated
- ¼ tsp dried parsley

Directions:

1. In a bowl, whisk eggs, ricotta cheese, garlic powder, parsley, cheese, and spinach.
2. Pour the egg mixture into each bell pepper half and top with mozzarella cheese.
3. Insert a crisper plate in the Ninja Foodi air fryer baskets.
4. Place bell peppers in both the baskets.
5. Select zone 1 then select "air fry" mode and set the temperature to 355 degrees F for 15 minutes. Press "match" to match zone 2 settings to zone 1. Press "start/stop" to begin.

Nutrition Info:

- (Per serving) Calories 136 | Fat 7.6g |Sodium 125mg | Carbs 6.9g | Fiber 0.9g | Sugar 3.5g | Protein 10.8g

Bagels

Servings: 8
Cooking Time: 15 Minutes
Ingredients:

- 2 cups self-rising flour
- 2 cups non-fat plain Greek yogurt
- 2 beaten eggs for egg wash (optional)
- ½ cup sesame seeds (optional)

Directions:

1. In a medium mixing bowl, combine the self-rising flour and Greek yogurt using a wooden spoon.
2. Knead the dough for about 5 minutes on a lightly floured board.
3. Divide the dough into four equal pieces and roll each into a thin rope, securing the ends to form a bagel shape.
4. Install a crisper plate in both drawers. Place 4 bagels in a single layer in each drawer. Insert the drawers into the unit.
5. Select zone 1, select AIR FRY, set temperature to 360 degrees F/ 180 degrees C, and set time to 15 minutes. Select MATCH to match zone 2 settings to zone 1. Select START/STOP to begin.
6. Once the timer has finished, remove the bagels from the units.
7. Serve and enjoy!

Nutrition Info:

- (Per serving) Calories 202 | Fat 4.5g | Sodium 55mg | Carbs 31.3g | Fiber 2.7g | Sugar 4.7g | Protein 8.7g

Blueberry Coffee Cake And Maple Sausage Patties

Servings:6
Cooking Time: 25 Minutes

Ingredients:

- FOR THE COFFEE CAKE
- 6 tablespoons unsalted butter, at room temperature, divided
- ⅓ cup granulated sugar
- 1 large egg
- 1 teaspoon vanilla extract
- ¼ cup whole milk
- 1½ cups all-purpose flour, divided
- 1 teaspoon baking powder
- ¼ teaspoon salt
- 1 cup blueberries
- ¼ cup packed light brown sugar
- ½ teaspoon ground cinnamon
- FOR THE SAUSAGE PATTIES
- ½ pound ground pork
- 2 tablespoons maple syrup
- ½ teaspoon dried sage
- ½ teaspoon dried thyme
- 1½ teaspoons kosher salt
- ½ teaspoon crushed fennel seeds
- ½ teaspoon red pepper flakes (optional)
- ¼ teaspoon freshly ground black pepper

Directions:

1. To prep the coffee cake: In a large bowl, cream together 4 tablespoons of butter with the granulated sugar. Beat in the egg, vanilla, and milk.
2. Stir in 1 cup of flour, along with the baking soda and salt, to form a thick batter. Fold in the blueberries.
3. In a second bowl, mix the remaining 2 tablespoons of butter, remaining ½ cup of flour, the brown sugar, and cinnamon to form a dry crumbly mixture.
4. To prep the sausage patties: In a large bowl, mix the pork, maple syrup, sage, thyme, salt, fennel seeds, red pepper flakes (if using), and black pepper until just combined.
5. Divide the mixture into 6 equal patties about ½ inch thick.
6. To cook the coffee cake and sausage patties: Spread the cake batter into the Zone 1 basket, top with the crumble mixture, and insert the basket in the unit. Install a crisper plate in the Zone 2 basket, add the sausage patties in a single layer, and insert the basket in the unit.
7. Select Zone 1, select BAKE, set the temperature to 350°F, and set the time to 25 minutes.
8. Select Zone 2, select AIR FRY, set the temperature to 375°F, and set the time to 12 minutes. Select SMART FINISH.
9. Press START/PAUSE to begin cooking.
10. When the Zone 2 timer reads 6 minutes, press START/PAUSE. Remove the basket and use silicone-tipped tongs to flip the sausage patties. Reinsert the basket and press START/PAUSE to resume cooking.
11. When cooking is complete, let the coffee cake cool for at least 5 minutes, then cut into 6 slices. Serve warm or at room temperature with the sausage patties.

Nutrition Info:

- (Per serving) Calories: 395; Total fat: 15g; Saturated fat: 8g; Carbohydrates: 53g; Fiber: 1.5g; Protein: 14g; Sodium: 187mg

Egg White Muffins

Servings: 8
Cooking Time: 10 Minutes

Ingredients:

- 4 slices center-cut bacon, cut into strips
- 4 ounces baby bella mushrooms, roughly chopped
- 2 ounces sun-dried tomatoes
- 2 tablespoon sliced black olives
- 2 tablespoons grated or shredded parmesan
- 2 tablespoons shredded mozzarella
- ¼ teaspoon black pepper
- ¾ cup liquid egg whites
- 2 tablespoons liquid egg whites

Directions:

1. Heat a saucepan with a little oil, add the bacon and mushrooms and cook until fully cooked and crispy, about 6–8 minutes.
2. While the bacon and mushrooms cook, mix the ¾ cup liquid egg whites, sun-dried tomato, olives, parmesan, mozzarella, and black pepper together in a large bowl.
3. Add the cooked bacon and mushrooms to the tomato and olive mixture, stirring everything together.
4. Spoon the mixture into muffin molds, followed by 2 tablespoons of egg whites over the top.
5. Place half the muffins mold in zone 1 and half in zone 2, then insert the drawers into the unit.
6. Select zone 1, select AIR FRY, set temperature to 390 degrees F/ 200 degrees C, and set time to 22 minutes.
7. Select MATCH to match zone 2 settings to zone 1. Press the START/STOP button to begin cooking.
8. When cooking is complete, remove the molds and enjoy!

Nutrition Info:

- (Per serving) Calories 104 | Fat 5.6g | Sodium 269mg | Carbs 3.5g | Fiber 0.8g | Sugar 0.3g | Protein 10.3g

Easy Pancake Doughnuts

Servings: 8
Cooking Time: 9 Minutes

Ingredients:

- 2 eggs
- 50g sugar
- 125ml vegetable oil
- 240g pancake mix
- 1 ½ tbsp cinnamon

Directions:

1. In a bowl, mix pancake mix, eggs, cinnamon, sugar, and oil until well combined.
2. Pour the doughnut mixture into the silicone doughnut moulds.
3. Insert a crisper plate in Ninja Foodi air fryer baskets.
4. Place doughnut moulds in both baskets.
5. Select zone 1 then select "air fry" mode and set the temperature to 355 degrees F for 9 minutes. Press "match" to match zone 2 settings to zone 1. Press "start/stop" to begin.

Nutrition Info:

- (Per serving) Calories 163 | Fat 14.7g |Sodium 16mg | Carbs 7.4g | Fiber 0.7g | Sugar 6.4g | Protein 1.4g

Air Fryer Sausage Patties

Servings: 12
Cooking Time: 10 Minutes
Ingredients:

- 1-pound pork sausage or ready-made patties
- Fennel seeds or preferred seasonings

Directions:

1. Prepare the sausage by slicing it into patties, then flavor it with fennel seed or your favorite seasonings.
2. Install a crisper plate in both drawers. Place half the patties in zone 1 and half in zone 2, then insert the drawers into the unit.
3. Select zone 1, select AIR FRY, set temperature to 390 degrees F/ 200 degrees C, and set time to 10 minutes.
4. Select MATCH to match zone 2 settings to zone 1.
5. Press the START/STOP button to begin cooking.
6. When cooking is complete, remove the patties from the unit and serve with sauce or make a burger.

Nutrition Info:

- (Per serving) Calories 130 | Fat 10.5g | Sodium 284mg | Carbs 0.3g | Fiber 0.2g | Sugar 0g | Protein 7.4g

Banana Muffins

Servings: 10
Cooking Time: 15 Minutes
Ingredients:

- 2 very ripe bananas
- ⅓ cup olive oil
- 1 egg
- ½ cup brown sugar
- 1 teaspoon vanilla extract
- 1 teaspoon cinnamon
- ¾ cup self-rising flour

Directions:

1. In a large mixing bowl, mash the bananas, then add the egg, brown sugar, olive oil, and vanilla. To blend, stir everything together thoroughly.
2. Fold in the flour and cinnamon until everything is just blended.
3. Fill muffin molds evenly with the mixture (silicone or paper).
4. Install a crisper plate in both drawers. Place the muffin molds in a single layer in each drawer. Insert the drawers into the unit.
5. Select zone 1, select AIR FRY, set temperature to 360 degrees F/ 180 degrees C, and set time to 15 minutes. Select MATCH to match zone 2 settings to zone 1. Select START/STOP to begin.
6. Once the timer has finished, remove the muffins from the drawers.
7. Serve and enjoy!

Nutrition Info:

- (Per serving) Calories 148 | Fat 7.3g | Sodium 9mg | Carbs 19.8g | Fiber 1g | Sugar 10g | Protein 1.8g

Pepper Egg Cups

Servings: 4
Cooking Time: 18 Minutes.

Ingredients:

- 2 halved bell pepper, seeds removed
- 4 eggs
- 1 teaspoon olive oil
- 1 pinch salt and black pepper
- 1 pinch sriracha flakes

Directions:

1. Slice the bell peppers in half, lengthwise, and remove their seeds and the inner portion to get a cup-like shape.
2. Rub olive oil on the edges of the bell peppers.
3. Place them in the two crisper plates with their cut side up and crack 1 egg in each half of bell pepper.
4. Drizzle salt, black pepper, and sriracha flakes on top of the eggs.
5. Return the crisper plates to the Ninja Foodi Dual Zone Air Fryer.
6. Choose the Air Fry mode for Zone 1 and set the temperature to 390 degrees F and the time to 18 minutes.
7. Select the "MATCH" button to copy the settings for Zone 2.
8. Initiate cooking by pressing the START/STOP button.
9. Serve warm and fresh.

Nutrition Info:

- (Per serving) Calories 183 | Fat 15g |Sodium 402mg | Carbs 2.5g | Fiber 0.4g | Sugar 1.1g | Protein 10g

Spinach And Red Pepper Egg Cups With Coffee-glazed Canadian Bacon

Servings:6
Cooking Time: 13 Minutes

Ingredients:

- FOR THE EGG CUPS
- 4 large eggs
- ¼ cup heavy (whipping) cream
- ¼ teaspoon kosher salt
- ¼ teaspoon freshly ground black pepper
- ½ cup roasted red peppers (about 1 whole pepper), drained and chopped
- ½ cup baby spinach, chopped
- FOR THE CANADIAN BACON
- ¼ cup brewed coffee
- 2 tablespoons maple syrup
- 1 tablespoon light brown sugar
- 6 slices Canadian bacon

Directions:

1. To prep the egg cups: In a medium bowl, whisk together the eggs and cream until well combined with a uniform, light color. Stir in the salt, black pepper, roasted red peppers, and spinach until combined.
2. Divide the egg mixture among 6 silicone muffin cups.
3. To prep the Canadian bacon: In a small bowl, whisk together the coffee, maple syrup, and brown sugar.
4. Using a basting brush, brush the glaze onto both sides of each slice of bacon.
5. To cook the egg cups and Canadian bacon: Install a crisper plate in each of the two baskets. Place the egg cups in the Zone 1 basket and insert the basket in the unit. Place the glazed bacon in the Zone 2 basket, making sure the slices don't overlap, and insert the basket in the unit. It is okay if the bacon overlaps a little bit.
6. Select Zone 1, select BAKE, set the temperature to 325°F, and set the time to 13 minutes.
7. Select Zone 2, select AIR FRY, set the temperature to 400°F, and set the time to 5 minutes. Select SMART FINISH.
8. Press START/PAUSE to begin cooking.
9. When the Zone 2 timer reads 2 minutes, press START/PAUSE. Remove the basket and use silicone-tipped tongs to flip the bacon. Reinsert the basket and press START/PAUSE to resume cooking.
10. When cooking is complete, serve the egg cups with the Canadian bacon.

Nutrition Info:

- (Per serving) Calories: 180; Total fat: 9.5g; Saturated fat: 4.5g; Carbohydrates: 9g; Fiber: 0g; Protein: 14g; Sodium: 688mg

Bacon And Egg Omelet

Servings:2
Cooking Time:10
Ingredients:

- 2 eggs, whisked
- ½ teaspoon of chopped tomatoes
- Sea Salt and black pepper, to taste
- 2 teaspoons of almond milk
-
- 1 teaspoon of cilantro, chopped
- 1 small green chili, chopped
- 4 slices of bacon

Directions:

1. Take a bowl and whisk eggs in it.
2. Then add green chili salt, black pepper, cilantro, almond milk, and chopped tomatoes.
3. Oil greases the ramekins.
4. Pour this into ramekins.
5. Put the bacon in the zone 1 basket and ramekins in zone 2 basket of the Ninja Foodie 2-Basket Air Fryer.
6. Now for zone 1, set it to AIR FRY mode at 400 degrees F for 10 minutes
7. And for zone 2, set it 350 degrees for 10 minutes in AIR FRY mode.
8. Press the Smart finish button and press start, it will finish both at the same time.
9. Once done, serve and enjoy.

Nutrition Info:

- (Per serving) Calories 285| Fat 21.5g| Sodium1000 mg | Carbs 2.2g | Fiber 0.1g| Sugar1 g | Protein 19.7g

Healthy Oatmeal Muffins

Servings: 6
Cooking Time: 17 Minutes
Ingredients:

- 1 egg
- ¼ tsp ground ginger
- 1 tsp ground cinnamon
- ½ tsp baking soda
- ½ tsp baking powder
- 55g brown sugar
- ½ tsp vanilla
- 2 tbsp butter, melted
- 125g applesauce
- 61ml milk
- 68gm whole wheat flour
- 100gm quick oats
- Pinch of salt

Directions:

1. In a mixing bowl, mix together all dry the ingredients.
2. In a separate bowl, add the remaining ingredients and mix well.
3. Add the dry ingredients mixture into the wet mixture and mix until well combined.
4. Pour the batter into the silicone muffin moulds.
5. Insert a crisper plate in the Ninja Foodi air fryer baskets.
6. Place muffin moulds in both baskets.
7. Select zone 1 then select "bake" mode and set the temperature to 390 degrees F for 17 minutes. Press "start/stop" to begin.

Nutrition Info:

- (Per serving) Calories 173 | Fat 5.8g |Sodium 177mg | Carbs 26.6g | Fiber 2.1g | Sugar 8.7g | Protein 4.2g

Lemon-cream Cheese Danishes Cherry Danishes

Servings:4
Cooking Time: 15 Minutes
Ingredients:

- FOR THE CREAM CHEESE DANISHES
- 1 ounce (2 tablespoons) cream cheese, at room temperature
- 1 teaspoon granulated sugar
- ¼ teaspoon freshly squeezed lemon juice
- ⅛ teaspoon vanilla extract
- ½ sheet frozen puff pastry, thawed
- 2 tablespoons lemon curd
- 1 large egg yolk
- 1 tablespoon water
- FOR THE CHERRY DANISHES
- ½ sheet frozen puff pastry, thawed
- 2 tablespoons cherry preserves
- 1 teaspoon coarse sanding sugar

Directions:

1. To prep the cream cheese Danishes: In a small bowl, mix the cream cheese, granulated sugar, lemon juice, and vanilla.
2. Cut the puff pastry sheet into 2 squares. Cut a ½-inch-wide strip from each side of the pastry. Brush the edges of the pastry square with water, then layer the strips along the edges, pressing gently to adhere and form a border around the outside of the pastry.
3. Divide the cream cheese mixture between the two pastries, then top each with 1 tablespoon of lemon curd.
4. In a second small bowl, whisk together the egg yolk and water (this will be used for the cherry Danishes, too). Brush the exposed edges of the pastry with half the egg wash.
5. To prep the cherry Danishes: Cut the puff pastry sheet into 2 squares. Cut a ½-inch-wide strip from each side of the pastry. Brush the edges of the pastry square with water, then layer the strips along the edges, pressing gently to adhere and form a border around the outside of the pastry.
6. Spoon 1 tablespoon of cherry preserves into the center of each pastry.
7. Brush the exposed edges of the pastry with the remaining egg wash, then sprinkle with the sanding sugar.
8. To cook both Danishes: Install a crisper plate in each of the two baskets. Place the cream cheese Danishes in the Zone 1 basket and insert the basket in the unit. Place the cherry Danishes in the Zone 2 basket and insert the basket in the unit.
9. Select Zone 1, select AIR FRY, set the temperature to 330°F, and set the time to 15 minutes. Select MATCH COOK to match Zone 2 settings to Zone 1.
10. Press START/PAUSE to begin cooking.
11. When cooking is complete, transfer the Danishes to a wire rack to cool. Serve warm.

Nutrition Info:

- (Per serving) Calories: 415; Total fat: 24g; Saturated fat: 12g; Carbohydrates: 51g; Fiber: 1.5g; Protein: 7g; Sodium: 274mg

Breakfast Stuffed Peppers

Servings: 4
Cooking Time: 13 Minutes
Ingredients:

- 2 capsicums, halved, seeds removed
- 4 eggs
- 1 teaspoon olive oil
- 1 pinch salt and pepper
- 1 pinch sriracha flakes

Directions:

1. Cut each capsicum in half and place two halves in each air fryer basket.
2. Crack one egg into each capsicum and top it with black pepper, salt, sriracha flakes and olive oil.
3. Return the air fryer basket 1 to Zone 1, and basket 2 to Zone 2 of the Ninja Foodi 2-Basket Air Fryer.
4. Choose the "Air Fry" mode for Zone 1 at 390 degrees F and 13 minutes of cooking time.
5. Select the "MATCH COOK" option to copy the settings for Zone 2.
6. Initiate cooking by pressing the START/PAUSE BUTTON.
7. Serve warm.

Nutrition Info:

- (Per serving) Calories 237 | Fat 19g |Sodium 518mg | Carbs 7g | Fiber 1.5g | Sugar 3.4g | Protein 12g

Honey Banana Oatmeal

Servings: 4
Cooking Time: 8 Minutes
Ingredients:

- 2 eggs
- 2 tbsp honey
- 1 tsp vanilla
- 45g quick oats
- 73ml milk
- 30g Greek yoghurt
- 219g banana, mashed

Directions:

1. In a bowl, mix eggs, milk, yoghurt, honey, vanilla, oats, and mashed banana until well combined.
2. Pour batter into the four greased ramekins.
3. Insert a crisper plate in the Ninja Foodi air fryer baskets.
4. Place ramekins in both baskets.
5. Select zone 1 then select "air fry" mode and set the temperature to 390 degrees F for 8 minutes. Press "match" to match zone 2 settings to zone 1. Press "start/stop" to begin.

Nutrition Info:

- (Per serving) Calories 228 | Fat 4.6g |Sodium 42mg | Carbs 40.4g | Fiber 4.2g | Sugar 16.1g | Protein 7.7g

Sweet Potato Hash

Servings: 4
Cooking Time: 15 Minutes
Ingredients:

- 3 sweet potatoes, peel & cut into ½-inch pieces
- ½ tsp cinnamon
- 2 tbsp olive oil
- 1 bell pepper, cut into ½-inch pieces
- ½ tsp dried thyme
- ½ tsp nutmeg
- 1 medium onion, cut into ½-inch pieces
- Pepper
- Salt

Directions:

1. In a bowl, toss sweet potatoes with the remaining ingredients.
2. Insert a crisper plate in Ninja Foodi air fryer baskets.
3. Add potato mixture in both baskets.
4. Select zone 1 then select "air fry" mode and set the temperature to 355 degrees F for 15 minutes. Press "match" to match zone 2 settings to zone 1. Press "start/stop" to begin.

Nutrition Info:

- (Per serving) Calories 167 | Fat 7.3g |Sodium 94mg | Carbs 24.9g | Fiber 4.2g | Sugar 6.8g | Protein 2.2g

Spinach Egg Muffins

Servings: 4

Cooking Time: 13 Minutes.

Ingredients:

- 4 tablespoons milk
- 4 tablespoons frozen spinach, thawed
- 4 large eggs
- 8 teaspoons grated cheese
-
- Salt, to taste
- Black pepper, to taste
- Cooking Spray

Directions:

1. Grease four small-sized ramekin with cooking spray.
2. Add egg, cheese, spinach, and milk to a bowl and beat well.
3. Divide the mixture into the four small ramekins and top them with salt and black pepper.
4. Place the two ramekins in each of the two crisper plate.
5. Return the crisper plate to the Ninja Foodi Dual Zone Air Fryer.
6. Choose the Air Fry mode for Zone 1 and set the temperature to 390 degrees F and the time to 13 minutes.
7. Select the "MATCH" button to copy the settings for Zone 2.
8. Initiate cooking by pressing the START/STOP button.
9. Serve warm.

Nutrition Info:

- (Per serving) Calories 237 | Fat 19g |Sodium 518mg | Carbs 7g | Fiber 1.5g | Sugar 3.4g | Protein 12g

Strawberry Baked Oats Chocolate Peanut Butter Baked Oats

Servings:12

Cooking Time: 15 Minutes

Ingredients:

- FOR THE STRAWBERRY OATS
- 1 cup whole milk
- 1 cup heavy (whipping) cream
- ½ cup maple syrup
- 2 teaspoons vanilla extract
- 2 large eggs
- 2 cups old-fashioned oats
- 2 teaspoons baking powder
- ½ teaspoon ground cinnamon
- ¼ teaspoon kosher salt
- 1½ cups diced strawberries
-
- FOR THE CHOCOLATE PEANUT BUTTER OATS
- 2 very ripe bananas
- ½ cup maple syrup
- ¼ cup unsweetened cocoa powder
- 2 teaspoons vanilla extract
- 2 teaspoons baking powder
- 2 large eggs
- ½ teaspoon kosher salt
- 2 cups old-fashioned oats
- 2 tablespoons peanut butter

Directions:

1. To prep the strawberry oats: In a large bowl, combine the milk, cream, maple syrup, vanilla, and eggs. Stir in the oats, baking powder, cinnamon, and salt until fully combined. Fold in the strawberries.
2. To prep the chocolate peanut butter oats: In a large bowl, mash the banana with a fork. Stir in the maple syrup, cocoa powder, vanilla, baking powder, and salt until smooth. Beat in the eggs. Stir in the oats until everything is combined.
3. To bake the oats: Place the strawberry oatmeal in the Zone 1 basket and insert the basket in the unit. Place the chocolate peanut butter oatmeal in the Zone 2 basket. Add ½ teaspoon dollops of peanut butter on top and insert the basket in the unit.
4. Select Zone 1, select BAKE, set the temperature to 320°F, and set the time to 15 minutes. Select MATCH COOK to match Zone 2 settings to Zone 1.
5. Press START/PAUSE to begin cooking.
6. When cooking is complete, serve each oatmeal in a shallow bowl.

Nutrition Info:

- (Per serving) Calories: 367; Total fat: 19g; Saturated fat: 11g; Carbohydrates: 42g; Fiber: 3.5g; Protein: 8g; Sodium: 102mg

Sausage & Butternut Squash

Servings: 2
Cooking Time: 20 Minutes

Ingredients:

- 450g butternut squash, diced
- 70g kielbasa, diced
- ¼ onion, diced
- ¼ tsp garlic powder
- ½ tbsp olive oil
- Pepper
- Salt

Directions:

1. In a bowl, toss butternut squash with garlic powder, oil, onion, kielbasa, pepper, and salt.
2. Insert a crisper plate in the Ninja Foodi air fryer baskets.
3. Add sausage and butternut squash mixture in both baskets.
4. Select zone 1, then select "air fry" mode and set the temperature to 375 degrees F for 20 minutes. Press "match" to match zone 2 settings to zone 1. Press "start/stop" to begin. Stir halfway through.

Nutrition Info:

- (Per serving) Calories 68 | Fat 3.6g |Sodium 81mg | Carbs 9.7g | Fiber 1.7g | Sugar 2.2g | Protein 0.9g

Breakfast Cheese Sandwich

Servings: 2
Cooking Time: 8 Minutes

Ingredients:

- 4 bread slices
- 2 provolone cheese slice
- ¼ tsp dried basil
- 2 tbsp mayonnaise
- 2 Monterey jack cheese slice
- 2 cheddar cheese slice
- ¼ tsp dried oregano

Directions:

1. In a small bowl, mix mayonnaise, basil, and oregano.
2. Spread mayonnaise on one side of the two bread slices.
3. Top two bread slices with cheddar cheese, provolone cheese, Monterey jack cheese slice, and cover with remaining bread slices.
4. Insert a crisper plate in the Ninja Foodi air fryer baskets.
5. Place sandwiches in both baskets.
6. Select zone 1, then select "air fry" mode and set the temperature to 390 degrees F for 8 minutes. Press "match" to match zone 2 settings to zone 1. Press "start/stop" to begin. Turn halfway through.

Nutrition Info:

- (Per serving) Calories 421 | Fat 30.7g |Sodium 796mg | Carbs 13.9g | Fiber 0.5g | Sugar 2.2g | Protein 22.5g

Roasted Oranges

Servings: 4
Cooking Time: 6 Minutes

Ingredients:

- 2 oranges, halved
- 2 teaspoons honey
- 1 teaspoon cinnamon

Directions:

1. Place the oranges in each air fryer basket.
2. Drizzle honey and cinnamon over the orange halves.
3. Return the air fryer basket 1 to Zone 1, and basket 2 to Zone 2 of the Ninja Foodi 2-Basket Air Fryer.
4. Choose the "Air Fry" mode for Zone 1 at 395 degrees F temperature and 6 minutes of cooking time.
5. Select the "MATCH COOK" option to copy the settings for Zone 2.
6. Initiate cooking by pressing the START/PAUSE BUTTON.
7. Serve.

Nutrition Info:

- (Per serving) Calories 183 | Fat 15g |Sodium 402mg | Carbs 2.5g | Fiber 0.4g | Sugar 1.1g | Protein 10g

Sausage Hash And Baked Eggs

Servings:4
Cooking Time: 30 Minutes

Ingredients:

- FOR THE HASH
- 2 yellow potatoes (about 1 pound), cut into ½-inch pieces
- 4 garlic cloves, minced
- 1 teaspoon kosher salt
- ¼ teaspoon freshly ground black pepper
- 2 tablespoons olive oil
- ½ pound pork breakfast sausage meat
-
- 1 small yellow onion, diced
- 1 red bell pepper, diced
- 1 teaspoon Italian seasoning
- FOR THE EGGS
- Nonstick cooking spray
- 4 large eggs
- 4 tablespoons water

Directions:

1. To prep the hash: In a large bowl, combine the potatoes, garlic, salt, black pepper, and olive oil and toss to coat. Crumble in the sausage and mix until combined.
2. To prep the eggs: Mist 4 silicone muffin cups with cooking spray. Crack 1 egg into each muffin cup. Top each egg with 1 tablespoon of water.
3. To cook the hash and eggs: Install a crisper plate in the Zone 1 basket. Place the sausage and potato mixture in the Zone 1 basket and insert the basket in the unit. Place the egg cups in the Zone 2 basket and insert the basket in the unit.
4. Select Zone 1, select AIR FRY, set the temperature to 400°F, and set the time to 30 minutes.
5. Select Zone 2, select BAKE, set the temperature to 325°F, and set the time to 12 minutes. Select SMART FINISH.
6. Press START/PAUSE to begin cooking.
7. When the Zone 1 timer reads 20 minutes, press START/PAUSE. Remove the basket and add the onion, bell pepper, and Italian seasoning to the hash. Mix until combined, breaking up any large pieces of sausage. Reinsert the basket and press START/PAUSE to resume cooking.
8. When cooking is complete, serve the hash topped with an egg.

Nutrition Info:

- (Per serving) Calories: 400; Total fat: 23g; Saturated fat: 5.5g; Carbohydrates: 31g; Fiber: 2g; Protein: 19g; Sodium: 750mg

Chapter 3 Snacks And Appetizers Recipes

Cheese Stuffed Mushrooms

Servings: 4
Cooking Time: 8 Minutes

Ingredients:

- 176g button mushrooms, clean & cut stems
- 46g sour cream
- 17g cream cheese, softened
- ½ tsp garlic powder
- 58g cheddar cheese, shredded
- Pepper
- Salt

Directions:

1. In a small bowl, mix cream cheese, garlic powder, sour cream, pepper, and salt.
2. Stuff cream cheese mixture into each mushroom and top each with cheddar cheese.
3. Insert a crisper plate in the Ninja Foodi air fryer baskets.
4. Place the stuffed mushrooms in both baskets.
5. Select zone 1 then select "air fry" mode and set the temperature to 370 degrees F for 8 minutes. Press "match" to match zone 2 settings to zone 1. Press "start/stop" to begin.

Nutrition Info:

- (Per serving) Calories 222 | Fat 19.4g |Sodium 220mg | Carbs 5.6g | Fiber 1.2g | Sugar 2.2g | Protein 8.9g

Crispy Chickpeas

Servings: 4
Cooking Time: 15 Minutes

Ingredients:

- 1 (15-ounce) can unsalted chickpeas, rinsed and drained
- 1½ tablespoons toasted sesame oil
- ¼ teaspoon smoked paprika
- ¼ teaspoon crushed red pepper
- ⅛ teaspoon salt
- Cooking spray
- 2 lime wedges

Directions:

1. The chickpeas should be spread out over multiple layers of paper towels. Roll the chickpeas under the paper towels to dry both sides, then top with more paper towels and pat until completely dry.
2. In a medium mixing bowl, combine the chickpeas and oil. Add the paprika, crushed red pepper, and salt to taste.
3. Place a crisper plate in each drawer. Put the chickpeas in a single layer in each drawer. Insert the drawers into the unit.
4. Select zone 1, then ROAST, then set the temperature to 400 degrees F/ 200 degrees C with a 15-minute timer. To match zone 2 settings to zone 1, choose MATCH. To begin, select START/STOP.

Nutrition Info:

- (Per serving) Calories 169 | Fat 5g | Sodium 357mg | Carbs 27.3g | Fiber 5.7g | Sugar 0.6g | Protein 5.9g

Parmesan Crush Chicken

Servings:4
Cooking Time:18
Ingredients:

- 4 chicken breasts
- 1 cup parmesan cheese
- 1 cup bread crumb
- 2 eggs, whisked
- Salt, to taste
- Oil spray, for greasing

Directions:

1. Whisk egg in a large bowl and set aside.
2. Season the chicken breast with salt and then put it in egg wash.
3. Next, dredge it in breadcrumb then parmesan cheese.
4. Line both the basket of the air fryer with parchment paper.
5. Divided the breast pieces between the backsets, and oil spray the breast pieces.
6. Set zone 1 basket to air fry mode at 350 degrees F for 18 minutes.
7. Select the MATCH button for the zone 2 basket.
8. Once it's done, serve.

Nutrition Info:

- (Per serving) Calories574 | Fat25g | Sodium848 mg | Carbs 21.4g | Fiber 1.2g| Sugar 1.8g | Protein 64.4g

Zucchini Chips

Servings: 4
Cooking Time: 15 Minutes
Ingredients:

- 1 medium-sized zucchini
- ½ cup panko breadcrumbs
- ½ teaspoon garlic powder
- ¼ teaspoon onion powder
- 1 egg
- 3 tablespoons flour

Directions:

1. Slice the zucchini into thin slices, about ¼-inch thick.
2. In a mixing bowl, combine the panko breadcrumbs, garlic powder, and onion powder.
3. The egg should be whisked in a different bowl, while the flour should be placed in a third bowl.
4. Dip the zucchini slices in the flour, then in the egg, and finally in the breadcrumbs.
5. Place a crisper plate in each drawer. Put the zucchini slices into each drawer in a single layer. Insert the drawers into the unit.
6. Select zone 1, then AIR FRY, then set the temperature to 360 degrees F/ 180 degrees C with a 6-minute timer. To match zone 2 settings to zone 1, choose MATCH. To begin, select START/STOP.
7. Remove the zucchini from the drawers after the timer has finished.

Nutrition Info:

- (Per serving) Calories 82 | Fat 1.5g | Sodium 89mg | Carbs 14.1g | Fiber 1.7g | Sugar 1.2g | Protein 3.9g

Potato Tater Tots

Servings: 4
Cooking Time: 27 Minutes.

Ingredients:

- 2 potatoes, peeled
- ½ teaspoon Cajun seasoning
- Olive oil cooking spray
- Sea salt to taste

Directions:

1. Boil water in a cooking pot and cook potatoes in it for 15 minutes.
2. Drain and leave the potatoes to cool in a bowl.
3. Grate these potatoes and toss them with Cajun seasoning.
4. Make small tater tots out of this mixture.
5. Divide them into the two crisper plates and spray them with cooking oil.
6. Return the crisper plates to the Ninja Foodi Dual Zone Air Fryer.
7. Choose the Air Fry mode for Zone 1 and set the temperature to 375 degrees F and the time to 27 minutes.
8. Select the "MATCH" button to copy the settings for Zone 2.
9. Initiate cooking by pressing the START/STOP button.
10. Flip them once cooked halfway through, and resume cooking.
11. Serve warm

Nutrition Info:

- (Per serving) Calories 185 | Fat 11g |Sodium 355mg | Carbs 21g | Fiber 5.8g | Sugar 3g | Protein 4.7g

Sweet Bites

Servings:4
Cooking Time:12

Ingredients:

- 10 sheets of Phyllo dough, (filo dough)
- 2 tablespoons of melted butter
- 1 cup walnuts, chopped
- 2 teaspoons of honey
- Pinch of cinnamon
- 1 teaspoon of orange zest

Directions:

1. First, layer together 10 Phyllo dough sheets on a flat surface.
2. Then cut it into 4 *4-inch squares.
3. Now, coat the squares with butter, drizzle some honey, orange zest, walnuts, and cinnamon.
4. Bring all 4 corners together and press the corners to make a little like purse design.
5. Divide it amongst air fryer basket and select zone 1 basket using AIR fry mode and set it for 7 minutes at 375 degrees F.
6. Select the MATCH button for the zone 2 basket.
7. Once done, take out and serve.

Nutrition Info:

- (Per serving) Calories 397| Fat 27.1 g| Sodium 271mg | Carbs31.2 g | Fiber 3.2g| Sugar3.3g | Protein 11g

Crab Cake Poppers

Servings: 6
Cooking Time: 10 Minutes
Ingredients:
- 1 egg, lightly beaten
- 453g lump crab meat, drained
- 1 tsp garlic, minced
- 1 tsp lemon juice
- 1 tsp old bay seasoning
- 30g almond flour
- 1 tsp Dijon mustard
- 28g mayonnaise
- Pepper
- Salt

Directions:
1. In a bowl, mix crab meat and remaining ingredients until well combined.
2. Make small balls from the crab meat mixture and place them on a plate.
3. Place the plate in the refrigerator for 50 minutes.
4. Insert a crisper plate in the Ninja Foodi air fryer baskets.
5. Place the prepared crab meatballs in both baskets.
6. Select zone 1 then select "air fry" mode and set the temperature to 360 degrees F for 10 minutes. Press "match" to match zone 2 settings to zone 1. Press "start/stop" to begin.

Nutrition Info:
- (Per serving) Calories 86 | Fat 8.5g |Sodium 615mg | Carbs 2.7g | Fiber 0.1g | Sugar 0.4g | Protein 12g

Fried Pickles

Servings: 4
Cooking Time: 15 Minutes
Ingredients:
- 2 cups sliced dill pickles
- 1 cup flour
- 1 tablespoon garlic powder
- 1 tablespoon Cajun spice
- ½ tablespoon cayenne pepper
- Olive Oil or cooking spray

Directions:
1. Mix together the flour and spices in a bowl.
2. Coat the sliced pickles with the flour mixture.
3. Place a crisper plate in each drawer. Put the pickles in a single layer in each drawer. Insert the drawers into the unit.
4. Select zone 1, then AIR FRY, then set the temperature to 400 degrees F/ 200 degrees C with a 15-minute timer. To match zone 2 settings to zone 1, choose MATCH. To begin, select START/STOP.

Nutrition Info:
- (Per serving) Calories 161 | Fat 4.1g | Sodium 975mg | Carbs 27.5g | Fiber 2.2g | Sugar 1.5g | Protein 4g

Crispy Popcorn Shrimp

Servings: 4
Cooking Time: 6 Minutes

Ingredients:

- 170g shrimp, peeled and diced
- ½ cup breadcrumbs
- Salt and black pepper to taste
- 2 eggs, beaten

Directions:

1. Mix breadcrumbs with black pepper and salt in a bowl.
2. Dip the shrimp pieces in the eggs and coat each with breadcrumbs.
3. Divide the shrimp popcorn into the 2 Air Fryer baskets.
4. Return the air fryer basket 1 to Zone 1, and basket 2 to Zone 2 of the Ninja Foodi 2-Basket Air Fryer.
5. Choose the "Air Fry" mode for Zone 1 at 400 degrees F and 6 minutes of cooking time.
6. Select the "MATCH COOK" option to copy the settings for Zone 2.
7. Initiate cooking by pressing the START/PAUSE BUTTON.
8. Serve warm.

Nutrition Info:

- (Per serving) Calories 180 | Fat 3.2g |Sodium 133mg | Carbs 32g | Fiber 1.1g | Sugar 1.8g | Protein 9g

Cheese Corn Fritters

Servings: 6
Cooking Time: 12 Minutes

Ingredients:

- 1 egg
- 164g corn
- 2 green onions, diced
- 45g flour
- 29g breadcrumbs
- 117g cheddar cheese, shredded
- ½ tsp onion powder
- ½ tsp garlic powder
- 15g sour cream
- Pepper
- Salt

Directions:

1. In a large bowl, add all ingredients and mix until well combined.
2. Insert a crisper plate in the Ninja Foodi air fryer baskets.
3. Make patties from the mixture and place them in both baskets.
4. Select zone 1, then select "air fry" mode and set the temperature to 370 degrees F for 12 minutes. Press "match" to match zone 2 settings to zone 1. Press "start/stop" to begin. Turn halfway through.

Nutrition Info:

- (Per serving) Calories 100 | Fat 4.8g |Sodium 135mg | Carbs 10g | Fiber 1.1g | Sugar 1.5g | Protein 5g

Ravioli

Servings: 2

Cooking Time: 6 Minutes

Ingredients:

- 12 frozen portions of ravioli
- ½ cup buttermilk
- ½ cup Italian breadcrumbs

Directions:

1. Place two bowls side by side. Put the buttermilk in one and breadcrumbs in the other.
2. Dip each piece of ravioli into the buttermilk then breadcrumbs, making sure to coat them as best as possible.
3. Place a crisper plate in both drawers. In each drawer, put four breaded ravioli pieces in a single layer. Insert the drawers into the unit.
4. Select zone 1, then AIR FRY, then set the temperature to 360 degrees F/ 180 degrees C with a 6-minute timer. To match zone 2 settings to zone 1, choose MATCH. To begin, select START/STOP.
5. Remove the ravioli from the drawers after the timer has finished.

Nutrition Info:

- (Per serving) Calories 481 | Fat 20g | Sodium 1162mg | Carbs 56g | Fiber 4g | Sugar 9g | Protein 19g

Beef Jerky Pineapple Jerky

Servings:8

Cooking Time: 6 To 12 Hours

Ingredients:

- FOR THE BEEF JERKY
- ½ cup reduced-sodium soy sauce
- ¼ cup pineapple juice
- 1 tablespoon dark brown sugar
- 1 tablespoon Worcestershire sauce
- ½ teaspoon smoked paprika
- ¼ teaspoon freshly ground black pepper
- ¼ teaspoon red pepper flakes
- 1 pound beef bottom round, trimmed of excess fat, cut into ¼-inch-thick slices
- FOR THE PINEAPPLE JERKY
- 1 pound pineapple, cut into ⅛-inch-thick rounds, pat dry
- 1 teaspoon chili powder (optional)

Directions:

1. To prep the beef jerky: In a large zip-top bag, combine the soy sauce, pineapple juice, brown sugar, Worcestershire sauce, smoked paprika, black pepper, and red pepper flakes.
2. Add the beef slices, seal the bag, and toss to coat the meat in the marinade. Refrigerate overnight or for at least 8 hours.
3. Remove the beef slices and discard the marinade. Using a paper towel, pat the slices dry to remove excess marinade.
4. To prep the pineapple jerky: Sprinkle the pineapple with chili powder (if using).
5. To dehydrate the jerky: Arrange half of the beef slices in a single layer in the Zone 1 basket, making sure they do not overlap. Place a crisper plate on top of the beef slices and arrange the remaining slices in a single layer on top of the crisper plate. Insert the basket in the unit.
6. Repeat this process with the pineapple in the Zone 2 basket and insert the basket in the unit.
7. Select Zone 1, select DEHYDRATE, set the temperature to 150°F, and set the time to 8 hours.
8. Select Zone 2, select DEHYDRATE, set the temperature to 135°F, and set the time to 12 hours.
9. Press START/PAUSE to begin cooking.
10. When the Zone 1 timer reads 2 hours, press START/PAUSE. Remove the basket and check the beef jerky for doneness. If necessary, reinsert the basket and press START/PAUSE to resume cooking.

Nutrition Info:

- (Per serving) Calories: 171; Total fat: 6.5g; Saturated fat: 2g; Carbohydrates: 2g; Fiber: 0g; Protein: 25g; Sodium: 369mg

Chili-lime Crispy Chickpeas Pizza-seasoned Crispy Chickpeas

Servings:6
Cooking Time: 20 Minutes

Ingredients:

- FOR THE CHILI-LIME CHICKPEAS
- 1½ cups canned chickpeas, rinsed and drained
- ¼ cup fresh lime juice
- 1 tablespoon olive oil
- 1½ teaspoons chili powder
- ½ teaspoon kosher salt
- FOR THE PIZZA-SEASONED CHICKPEAS
- 1½ cups canned chickpeas, rinsed and drained
- 1 tablespoon olive oil
-
- 1 tablespoon grated Parmesan cheese
- ½ teaspoon dried basil
- ½ teaspoon dried oregano
- ½ teaspoon kosher salt
- ¼ teaspoon onion powder
- ¼ teaspoon garlic powder
- ¼ teaspoon fennel seeds
- ¼ teaspoon dried thyme
- ¼ teaspoon red pepper flakes (optional)

Directions:

1. To prep the chili-lime chickpeas: In a small bowl, mix the chickpeas, lime juice, olive oil, chili powder, and salt until the chickpeas are well coated.
2. To prep the pizza-seasoned chickpeas: In a small bowl, mix the chickpeas, olive oil, Parmesan, basil, oregano, salt, onion powder, garlic powder, fennel, thyme, and red pepper flakes (if using) until the chickpeas are well coated.
3. To cook the chickpeas: Install a crisper plate in each of the two baskets. Place the chili-lime chickpeas in the Zone 1 basket and insert the basket in the unit. Place the pizza-seasoned chickpeas in the Zone 2 basket and insert the basket in the unit.
4. Select Zone 1, select AIR FRY, set the temperature to 375°F, and set the time to 20 minutes. Select MATCH COOK to match Zone 2 settings to Zone 1.
5. Press START/PAUSE to begin cooking.
6. When both timers read 10 minutes, press START/PAUSE. Remove both baskets and give each basket a shake to redistribute the chickpeas. Reinsert both baskets and press START/PAUSE to resume cooking.
7. When both timers read 5 minutes, press START/PAUSE. Remove both baskets and give each basket a good shake again. Reinsert both baskets and press START/PAUSE to resume cooking.
8. When cooking is complete, the chickpeas will be crisp and golden brown. Serve warm or at room temperature.

Nutrition Info:

- (Per serving) Calories: 145; Total fat: 6.5g; Saturated fat: 0.5g; Carbohydrates: 17g; Fiber: 4.5g; Protein: 5g; Sodium: 348mg

Onion Rings

Servings: 4
Cooking Time: 7 Minutes

Ingredients:

- 170g onion, sliced into rings
- ½ cup breadcrumbs
- 2 eggs, beaten
-
- ½ cup flour
- Salt and black pepper to taste

Directions:

1. Mix flour, black pepper and salt in a bowl.
2. Dredge the onion rings through the flour mixture.
3. Dip them in the eggs and coat with the breadcrumbs.
4. Place the coated onion rings in the air fryer baskets.
5. Return the air fryer basket 1 to Zone 1, and basket 2 to Zone 2 of the Ninja Foodi 2-Basket Air Fryer.
6. Choose the "Air Fry" mode for Zone 1 at 350 degrees F and 7 minutes of cooking time.
7. Select the "MATCH COOK" option to copy the settings for Zone 2.
8. Initiate cooking by pressing the START/PAUSE BUTTON.
9. Shake the rings once cooked halfway through.
10. Serve warm.

Nutrition Info:

- (Per serving) Calories 185 | Fat 11g |Sodium 355mg | Carbs 21g | Fiber 5.8g | Sugar 3g | Protein 4.7g

Jalapeño Popper Chicken

Servings: 4
Cooking Time: 50 Minutes

Ingredients:

- 2 ounces cream cheese, softened
- ¼ cup shredded cheddar cheese
- ¼ cup shredded mozzarella cheese
- ¼ teaspoon garlic powder
- 4 small jalapeño peppers, seeds removed and diced
- Kosher salt, as desired
- Ground black pepper, as desired
- 4 organic boneless, skinless chicken breasts
- 8 slices bacon

Directions:

1. Cream together the cream cheese, cheddar cheese, mozzarella cheese, garlic powder, and jalapeño in a mixing bowl. Add salt and pepper to taste.
2. Make a deep pocket in the center of each chicken breast, but be cautious not to cut all the way through.
3. Fill each chicken breast's pocket with the cream cheese mixture.
4. Wrap two strips of bacon around each chicken breast and attach them with toothpicks.
5. Place a crisper plate in each drawer. Put the chicken breasts in the drawers. Place both drawers in the unit.
6. Select zone 1, then AIR FRY, and set the temperature to 350 degrees F/ 175 degrees C with a 30-minute timer. To match zone 2 and zone 1 settings, select MATCH. To begin cooking, press the START/STOP button.
7. When cooking is complete, remove the chicken breasts and allow them to rest for 5 minutes before serving

Nutrition Info:

- (Per serving) Calories 507 | Fat 27.5g | Sodium 1432mg | Carbs 2.3g | Fiber 0.6g | Sugar 0.6g | Protein 58.2g

Chicken Crescent Wraps

Servings: 6
Cooking Time: 12 Minutes.

Ingredients:

- 3 tablespoons chopped onion
- 3 garlic cloves, peeled and minced
- ¾ (8 ounces) package cream cheese
-
- 6 tablespoons butter
- 2 boneless chicken breasts, cubed, cooked
- 3 (10 ounces) cans refrigerated crescent roll dough

Directions:

1. Heat oil in a skillet and add onion and garlic to sauté until soft.
2. Add cooked chicken, sautéed veggies, butter, and cream cheese to a blender.
3. Blend well until smooth. Spread the crescent dough over a flat surface.
4. Slice the dough into 12 rectangles.
5. Spoon the chicken mixture at the center of each rectangle.
6. Roll the dough to wrap the mixture and form a ball.
7. Divide these balls into the two crisper plate.
8. Return the crisper plate to the Ninja Foodi Dual Zone Air Fryer.
9. Choose the Air Fry mode for Zone 1 and set the temperature to 390 degrees F and the time to 12 minutes.
10. Select the "MATCH" button to copy the settings for Zone 2.
11. Initiate cooking by pressing the START/STOP button.
12. Serve warm.

Nutrition Info:

- (Per serving) Calories 100 | Fat 2g |Sodium 480mg | Carbs 4g | Fiber 2g | Sugar 0g | Protein 18g

Chicken Stuffed Mushrooms

Servings: 6
Cooking Time: 15 Minutes.

Ingredients:

- 6 large fresh mushrooms, stems removed
- Stuffing:
- ½ cup chicken meat, cubed
- 1 (4 ounces) package cream cheese, softened
- ¼ lb. imitation crabmeat, flaked
- 1 cup butter
- 1 garlic clove, peeled and minced
- Black pepper and salt to taste
- Garlic powder to taste
- Crushed red pepper to taste

Directions:

1. Melt and heat butter in a skillet over medium heat.
2. Add chicken and sauté for 5 minutes.
3. Add in all the remaining ingredients for the stuffing.
4. Cook for 5 minutes, then turn off the heat.
5. Allow the mixture to cool. Stuff each mushroom with a tablespoon of this mixture.
6. Divide the stuffed mushrooms in the two crisper plates.
7. Return the crisper plate to the Ninja Foodi Dual Zone Air Fryer.
8. Choose the Air Fry mode for Zone 1 and set the temperature to 375 degrees F and the time to 15 minutes.
9. Select the "MATCH" button to copy the settings for Zone 2.
10. Initiate cooking by pressing the START/STOP button.
11. Serve warm.

Nutrition Info:

- (Per serving) Calories 180 | Fat 3.2g |Sodium 133mg | Carbs 32g | Fiber 1.1g | Sugar 1.8g | Protein 9g

Buffalo Wings Honey-garlic Wings

Servings:6

Cooking Time: 40 Minutes

Ingredients:

- FOR THE BUFFALO WINGS
- 2 pounds chicken wings
- ¼ teaspoon kosher salt
- ¼ teaspoon freshly ground black pepper
- ¼ teaspoon paprika
- 1 tablespoon vegetable oil
- ⅓ cup Buffalo wing sauce
- FOR THE HONEY-GARLIC WINGS
-
- 2 pounds chicken wings
- 2 tablespoons all-purpose flour
- ½ teaspoon garlic powder
- 1 tablespoon vegetable oil
- ¼ cup honey
- 2 tablespoons reduced-sodium soy sauce
- ½ teaspoon ground ginger (optional)

Directions:

1. To prep the Buffalo wings: In a large bowl, combine the wings, salt, black pepper, and paprika and toss to coat the wings with the seasonings. Drizzle with the oil.
2. To prep the honey-garlic wings: In another large bowl, combine the wings, flour, and garlic powder and toss to coat the wings. Drizzle with the oil.
3. In a small bowl, whisk together the honey, soy sauce, and ginger (if using). Set the honey-soy sauce aside.
4. To cook the wings: Install a crisper plate in each of the two baskets. Place the Buffalo wings in the Zone 1 basket and insert the basket in the unit. Place the honey-garlic wings in the Zone 2 basket and insert the basket in the unit.
5. Select Zone 1, select AIR FRY, set the temperature to 390°F, and set the time to 40 minutes. Select MATCH COOK to match Zone 2 settings to Zone 1.
6. Press START/PAUSE to begin cooking.
7. When both timers read 8 minutes, press START/PAUSE. Remove the Zone 1 basket, drizzle the Buffalo sauce over the wings, and shake to coat the wings with the sauce. Reinsert the basket. Remove the Zone 2 basket, drizzle the honey-soy sauce over the wings, and shake to coat the wings with the sauce. Reinsert the basket. Press START/PAUSE to resume cooking.
8. When cooking is complete, the wings will be golden brown and cooked through. Use silicone-tipped tongs to transfer the wings to a serving plate. Serve warm.

Nutrition Info:

- (Per serving) Calories: 399; Total fat: 28g; Saturated fat: 7.5g; Carbohydrates: 0g; Fiber: 0g; Protein: 34g; Sodium: 1,049mg

Tater Tots

Servings: 4

Cooking Time: 8 Minutes

Ingredients:

- 16 ounces tater tots
- ½ cup shredded cheddar cheese
- 1½ teaspoons bacon bits
- 2 green onions, chopped
- Sour cream (optional)

Directions:

1. Place a crisper plate in each drawer. Put the tater tots into the drawers in a single layer. Insert the drawers into the unit.
2. Select zone 1, then AIR FRY, then set the temperature to 360 degrees F/ 180 degrees C with a 6-minute timer. To match zone 2 settings to zone 1, choose MATCH. To begin, select START/STOP.
3. When the cooking time is over, add the shredded cheddar cheese, bacon bits, and green onions over the tater tots. Select zone 1, AIR FRY, 360 degrees F/ 180 degrees C, for 4 minutes. Select MATCH. Press START/STOP.
4. Drizzle sour cream over the top before serving.
5. Enjoy!

Nutrition Info:

- (Per serving) Calories 335 | Fat 19.1g | Sodium 761mg | Carbs 34.1g | Fiber 3g | Sugar 0.6g | Protein 8.9g

Mac And Cheese Balls

Servings: 4
Cooking Time: 20 Minutes
Ingredients:

- 1 cup panko breadcrumbs
- 4 cups prepared macaroni and cheese, refrigerated
- 3 tablespoons flour
- 1 teaspoon salt, divided
- 1 teaspoon ground black pepper, divided
- 1 teaspoon smoked paprika, divided
- ½ teaspoon garlic powder, divided
- 2 eggs
- 1 tablespoon milk
- ¼ cup ranch dressing, garlic aioli, or chipotle mayo, for dipping (optional)
-

Directions:

1. Preheat a conventional oven to 400 degrees F/ 200 degrees C.
2. Shake the breadcrumbs onto a baking sheet so that they're evenly distributed. Bake in the oven for 3 minutes, then shake and bake for an additional 1 to 2 minutes, or until toasted.
3. Form the chilled macaroni and cheese into golf ball-sized balls and set them aside.
4. Combine the flour, ½ teaspoon salt, ½ teaspoon black pepper, ½ teaspoon smoked paprika, and ¼ teaspoon garlic powder in a large mixing bowl.
5. In a small bowl, whisk together the eggs and milk.
6. Combine the breadcrumbs, remaining salt, pepper, paprika, and garlic powder in a mixing bowl.
7. To coat the macaroni and cheese balls, roll them in the flour mixture, then the egg mixture, and then the breadcrumb mixture.
8. Place a crisper plate in each drawer. Put the cheese balls in a single layer in each drawer. Insert the drawers into the unit.
9. Select zone 1, then AIR FRY, then set the temperature to 360 degrees F/ 180 degrees C with an 8-minute timer. To match zone 2 settings to zone 1, choose MATCH. To begin, select START/STOP.
10. Serve and enjoy!

Nutrition Info:

- (Per serving) Calories 489 | Fat 15.9g | Sodium 1402mg | Carbs 69.7g | Fiber 2.5g | Sugar 4g | Protein 16.9g

Stuffed Mushrooms

Servings: 5
Cooking Time: 8 Minutes
Ingredients:

- 8 ounces fresh mushrooms (I used Monterey)
- 4 ounces cream cheese
- ¼ cup shredded parmesan cheese
- ⅛cup shredded sharp cheddar cheese
- ⅛ cup shredded white cheddar cheese
- 1 teaspoon Worcestershire sauce
- 2 garlic cloves, minced
- Salt and pepper, to taste
-

Directions:

1. To prepare the mushrooms for stuffing, remove their stems. Make a circle cut around the area where the stem used to be. Continue to cut until all of the superfluous mushroom is removed.
2. To soften the cream cheese, microwave it for 15 seconds.
3. Combine the cream cheese, shredded cheeses, salt, pepper, garlic, and Worcestershire sauce in a medium mixing bowl. To blend, stir everything together.
4. Stuff the mushrooms with the cheese mixture.
5. Place a crisper plate in each drawer. Put the stuffed mushrooms in a single layer in each drawer. Insert the drawers into the unit.
6. Select zone 1, then AIR FRY, then set the temperature to 360 degrees F/ 180 degrees C with an 8-minute timer. To match zone 2 settings to zone 1, choose MATCH. To begin, select START/STOP.
7. Serve and enjoy!

Nutrition Info:

- (Per serving) Calories 230 | Fat 9.5g | Sodium 105mg | Carbs 35.5g | Fiber 5.1g | Sugar 0.1g | Protein 7.1g

Spicy Chicken Tenders

Servings:2
Cooking Time:12
Ingredients:

- 2 large eggs, whisked
- 2 tablespoons lemon juice
- Salt and black pepper
- 1 pound of chicken tenders
- 1 cup Panko breadcrumbs
- 1/2 cup Italian bread crumb
- 1 teaspoon smoked paprika
- 1/4 teaspoon garlic powder
- 1/4 teaspoon onion powder
- 1/2 cup fresh grated parmesan cheese

Directions:

1. Take a bowl and whisk eggs in it and set aside for further use.
2. In a large bowl add lemon juice, paprika, salt, black pepper, garlic powder, onion powder
3. In a separate bowl mix Panko breadcrumbs, Italian bread crumbs, and parmesan cheese.
4. Dip the chicken tender in the spice mixture and coat the entire tender well.
5. Let the tenders sit for 1 hour.
6. Then dip each chicken tender in egg and then in bread crumbs.
7. Line both the basket of the air fryer with parchment paper.
8. Divide the tenders between the baskets.
9. Set zone 1 basket to air fry mode at 350 degrees F for 12 minutes.
10. Select the MATCH button for the zone 2 basket.
11. Once it's done, serve.

Nutrition Info:

- (Per serving) Calories 836| Fat 36g| Sodium1307 mg | Carbs 31.3g | Fiber 2.5g| Sugar3.3 g | Protein 95.3g

Healthy Chickpea Fritters

Servings: 6
Cooking Time: 5 Minutes
Ingredients:

- 1 egg
- 425g can chickpeas, rinsed & drained
- ½ tsp ground ginger
- ½ tsp garlic powder
- 1 tsp ground cumin
- 2 green onions, sliced
- 15g fresh cilantro, chopped
- ½ tsp baking soda
- ½ tsp salt

Directions:

1. Add chickpeas and remaining ingredients into the food processor and process until well combined.
2. Insert a crisper plate in the Ninja Foodi air fryer baskets.
3. Make patties from the mixture and place them in both baskets.
4. Select zone 1, then select "air fry" mode and set the temperature to 390 degrees F for 5 minutes. Press "match" to match zone 2 settings to zone 1. Press "start/stop" to begin.

Nutrition Info:

- (Per serving) Calories 94 | Fat 1.6g |Sodium 508mg | Carbs 15.9g | Fiber 3.2g | Sugar 0.3g | Protein 4.4g

Healthy Spinach Balls

Servings: 4
Cooking Time: 10 Minutes

Ingredients:

- 1 egg
- 29g breadcrumbs
- ½ medium onion, chopped
- 225g spinach, blanched & chopped
- 1 carrot, peel & grated
- 1 tbsp cornflour
- 1 tbsp nutritional yeast
- 1 tsp garlic, minced
- ½ tsp garlic powder
- Pepper
- Salt

Directions:

1. Add spinach and remaining ingredients into the mixing bowl and mix until well combined.
2. Insert a crisper plate in the Ninja Foodi air fryer baskets.
3. Make small balls from the spinach mixture and place them in both baskets.
4. Select zone 1, then select "air fry" mode and set the temperature to 390 degrees F for 10 minutes. Press "match" to match zone 2 settings to zone 1. Press "start/stop" to begin.

Nutrition Info:

- (Per serving) Calories 74 | Fat 1.7g |Sodium 122mg | Carbs 11.1g | Fiber 1.9g | Sugar 2g | Protein 4.2g

Tasty Sweet Potato Wedges

Servings: 4
Cooking Time: 20 Minutes

Ingredients:

- 2 sweet potatoes, peel & cut into wedges
- 1 tbsp BBQ spice rub
- ½ tsp sweet paprika
- 1 tbsp olive oil
- Pepper
- Salt

Directions:

1. In a bowl, toss sweet potato wedges with sweet paprika, oil, BBQ spice rub, pepper, and salt.
2. Insert a crisper plate in the Ninja Foodi air fryer baskets.
3. Add sweet potato wedges in both baskets.
4. Select zone 1 then select "air fry" mode and set the temperature to 390 degrees F for 20 minutes. Press "match" to match zone 2 settings to zone 1. Press "start/stop" to begin. Turn halfway through.

Nutrition Info:

- (Per serving) Calories 87 | Fat 3.6g |Sodium 75mg | Carbs 13.2g | Fiber 2.1g | Sugar 2.8g | Protein 1.1g

Chapter 4 Beef, Pork, And Lamb Recipes

Pork Chops And Potatoes

Servings: 3
Cooking Time: 12 Minutes

Ingredients:

- 455g red potatoes
- Olive oil
- Salt and pepper
- 1 teaspoon garlic powder
- 1 teaspoon fresh rosemary, chopped
-
- 2 tablespoons brown sugar
- 1 tablespoon soy sauce
- 1 tablespoon Worcestershire sauce
- 1 teaspoon lemon juice
- 3 small pork chops

Directions:

1. Mix potatoes and pork chops with remaining ingredients in a bowl.
2. Divide the ingredients in the air fryer baskets.
3. Return the air fryer basket 1 to Zone 1, and basket 2 to Zone 2 of the Ninja Foodi 2-Basket Air Fryer.
4. Choose the "Air Fry" mode for Zone 1 at 400 degrees F and 12 minutes of cooking time.
5. Select the "MATCH COOK" option to copy the settings for Zone 2.
6. Initiate cooking by pressing the START/PAUSE BUTTON.
7. Flip the chops and toss potatoes once cooked halfway through.
8. Serve warm.

Nutrition Info:

- (Per serving) Calories 352 | Fat 9.1g |Sodium 1294mg | Carbs 3.9g | Fiber 1g | Sugar 1g | Protein 61g

Gochujang Brisket

Servings: 6
Cooking Time: 55 Minutes.

Ingredients:

- ½ tablespoons sweet paprika
- ½ teaspoon toasted sesame oil
- 2 lbs. beef brisket, cut into 4 pieces
- Salt, to taste
- ⅛ cup Gochujang, Korean chili paste
- Black pepper, to taste
- 1 small onion, diced
- 2 garlic cloves, minced
-
- 1 teaspoon Asian fish sauce
- 1 ½ tablespoons peanut oil, as needed
- ½ tablespoon fresh ginger, grated
- ¼ teaspoon red chili flakes
- ½ cup of water
- 1 tablespoon ketchup
- 1 tablespoon soy sauce

Directions:

1. Thoroughly rub the beef brisket with olive oil, paprika, chili flakes, black pepper, and salt.
2. Cut the brisket in half, then divide the beef in the two crisper plate.
3. Return the crisper plate to the Ninja Foodi Dual Zone Air Fryer.
4. Choose the Air Fry mode for Zone 1 and set the temperature to 390 degrees F and the time to 35 minutes.
5. Select the "MATCH" button to copy the settings for Zone 2.
6. Initiate cooking by pressing the START/STOP button.
7. Flip the brisket halfway through, and resume cooking.
8. Meanwhile, heat oil in a skillet and add ginger, onion, and garlic.
9. Sauté for 5 minutes, then add all the remaining ingredients.
10. Cook the mixture for 15 minutes approximately until well thoroughly mixed.
11. Serve the brisket with this sauce on top.

Nutrition Info:

- (Per serving) Calories 374 | Fat 25g |Sodium 275mg | Carbs 7.3g | Fiber 0g | Sugar 6g | Protein 12.3g

Yogurt Lamb Chops

Servings:2
Cooking Time:20

Ingredients:

- 1½ cups plain Greek yogurt
- 1 lemon, juice only
- 1 teaspoon ground cumin
- 1 teaspoon ground coriander
-
- ¾teaspoon ground turmeric
- ¼ teaspoon ground allspice
- 10 rib lamb chops (1–1¼ inches thick cut)
- 2 tablespoons olive oil, divided

Directions:

1. Take a bowl and add lamb chop along with listed ingredients.
2. Rub the lamb chops well.
3. and let it marinate in the refrigerator for 1 hour.
4. Afterward takeout the lamb chops from the refrigerator.
5. Layer parchment paper on top of the baskets of the air fryer.
6. Divide it between ninja air fryer baskets.
7. Set the time for zone 1 to 20 minutes at 400 degrees F.
8. Select the MATCH button for the zone 2 basket.
9. Hit start and then wait for the chop to be cooked.
10. Once the cooking is done, the cool sign will appear on display.
11. Take out the lamb chops and let the chops serve on plates.

Nutrition Info:

- (Per serving) Calories1973 | Fat90 g| Sodium228 mg | Carbs 109.2g | Fiber 1g | Sugar 77.5g | Protein 184g

Tomahawk Steak

Servings: 4
Cooking Time: 12 Minutes

Ingredients:

- 4 tablespoons butter, softened
- 2 cloves garlic, minced
- 2 teaspoons chopped fresh parsley
- 1 teaspoon chopped chives
- 1 teaspoon chopped fresh thyme
- 1 teaspoon chopped fresh rosemary
- 2 (2 pounds each) bone-in ribeye steaks
- Kosher salt, to taste
- Freshly ground black pepper, to taste

Directions:

1. In a small bowl, combine the butter and herbs. Place the mixture in the center of a piece of plastic wrap and roll it into a log. Twist the ends together to keep it tight and refrigerate until hardened, about 20 minutes.
2. Season the steaks on both sides with salt and pepper.
3. Install a crisper plate in both drawers. Place one steak in the zone 1 drawer and one in zone 2's, then insert the drawers into the unit.
4. Select zone 1, select AIR FRY, set temperature to 390 degrees F/ 200 degrees C, and set time to 12 minutes. Select MATCH to match zone 2 settings to zone 1. Press the START/STOP button to begin cooking.
5. When the time reaches 10 minutes, press START/STOP to pause the unit. Remove the drawers and flip the steaks. Add the herb-butter to the tops of the steaks. Re-insert the drawers into the unit and press START/STOP to resume cooking.
6. Serve and enjoy!

Nutrition Info:

- (Per serving) Calories 338 | Fat 21.2g | Sodium 1503mg | Carbs 5.1g | Fiber 0.3g | Sugar 4.6g | Protein 29.3g

Steak Fajitas With Onions And Peppers

Servings: 6
Cooking Time: 15 Minutes

Ingredients:

- 1 pound steak
- 1 green bell pepper, sliced
- 1 yellow bell pepper, sliced
- 1 red bell pepper, sliced
- ½ cup sliced white onions
- 1 packet gluten-free fajita seasoning
- Olive oil spray

Directions:

1. Thinly slice the steak against the grain. These should be about ¼-inch slices.
2. Mix the steak with the peppers and onions.
3. Evenly coat with the fajita seasoning.
4. Install a crisper plate in both drawers. Place half the steak mixture in the zone 1 drawer and half in zone 2's, then insert the drawers into the unit.
5. Select zone 1, select AIR FRY, set temperature to 390 degrees F/ 200 degrees C, and set time to 15 minutes. Select MATCH to match zone 2 settings to zone 1. Press the START/STOP button to begin cooking.
6. When the time reaches 10 minutes, press START/STOP to pause the unit. Remove the drawers and flip the steak strips. Re-insert the drawers into the unit and press START/STOP to resume cooking.
7. Serve in warm tortillas.

Nutrition Info:

- (Per serving) Calories 305 | Fat 17g | Sodium 418mg | Carbs 15g | Fiber 2g | Sugar 4g | Protein 22g

Short Ribs & Root Vegetables

Servings:2
Cooking Time:45

Ingredients:

- 1 pound of beef short ribs, bone-in and trimmed
- Salt and black pepper, to taste
- 2 tablespoons canola oil, divided
- 1/4 cup red wine
- 3 tablespoons brown sugar
- 2 cloves garlic, peeled, minced
- 4 carrots, peeled, cut into 1-inch pieces
- 2 parsnips, peeled, cut into 1-inch pieces
- ½ cup pearl onions

Directions:

1. Season the ribs with salt and black pepper and rub a little amount of canola oil on both sides.
2. Place it in zone 1 basket of the air fryer.
3. Next, take a bowl and add pearl onions, parsnip, carrots, garlic, brown sugar, red wine, salt, and black pepper.
4. Add the vegetable mixture to the zone 2 basket.
5. Set the zone 1 basket time to 12 minutes at 375 degrees F at AIR FRY mode.
6. Set the zone 2 basket at AIR FRY mode at 390 degrees F for 18 minutes.
7. Hit start so the cooking cycle being.
8. Once the cooking complete, take out the ingredient and serve short ribs with the mixed vegetables and liquid collect at the bottom of zone 2 basket
9. Enjoy it hot.

Nutrition Info:

- (Per serving) Calories1262 | Fat 98.6g| Sodium 595mg | Carbs 57g | Fiber 10.1g| Sugar 28.2g | Protein 35.8g

Beef And Bean Taquitos With Mexican Rice

Servings:4
Cooking Time: 15 Minutes
Ingredients:

- FOR THE TAQUITOS
- ½ pound ground beef (85 percent lean)
- 1 tablespoon taco seasoning
- 8 (6-inch) soft white corn tortillas
- Nonstick cooking spray
- ¾ cup canned refried beans
- ½ cup shredded Mexican blend cheese (optional)
- FOR THE MEXICAN RICE
- 1 cup dried instant white rice (not microwavable)
- 1½ cups chicken broth
- ¼ cup jarred salsa
- 2 tablespoons canned tomato sauce
- 1 tablespoon vegetable oil
- ½ teaspoon kosher salt

Directions:

1. To prep the taquitos: In a large bowl, mix the ground beef and taco seasoning until well combined.
2. Mist both sides of each tortilla lightly with cooking spray.
3. To prep the Mexican rice: In the Zone 2 basket, combine the rice, broth, salsa, tomato sauce, oil, and salt. Stir well to ensure all of the rice is submerged in the liquid.
4. To cook the taquitos and rice: Install a crisper plate in the Zone 1 basket. Place the seasoned beef in the basket and insert the basket in the unit. Insert the Zone 2 basket in the unit.
5. Select Zone 1, select AIR FRY, set the temperature to 390°F, and set the time to 15 minutes.
6. Select Zone 2, select BAKE, set the temperature to 350°F, and set the time to 10 minutes. Select SMART FINISH.
7. Press START/PAUSE to begin cooking.
8. When the Zone 1 timer reads 10 minutes, press START/PAUSE. Remove the basket and transfer the beef to a medium bowl. Add the refried beans and cheese (if using) and combine well. Spoon 2 tablespoons of the filling onto each tortilla and roll tightly. Place the taquitos in the Zone 1 basket seam-side down. Reinsert the basket in the unit and press START/PAUSE to resume cooking.
9. When cooking is complete, the taquitos should be crisp and golden brown and the rice cooked through. Serve hot.

Nutrition Info:

- (Per serving) Calories: 431; Total fat: 18g; Saturated fat: 4g; Carbohydrates: 52g; Fiber: 5.5g; Protein: 18g; Sodium: 923mg

Steak Bites With Cowboy Butter

Servings: 4
Cooking Time: 15 Minutes
Ingredients:

- 455g steak sirloin
- Cooking spray
- Cowboy butter sauce
- 1 stick salted butter melted
- 1 tablespoon lemon zest
- 1 tablespoon lemon juice
- ½ teaspoon garlic powder
-
- ¼ teaspoon red pepper flakes
- ½ teaspoon sea salt
- ½ teaspoon black pepper
- ½ tablespoon Dijon mustard
- ½ teaspoon Worcestershire sauce
- 1 tablespoon parsley freshly chopped

Directions:

1. Mix all the cowboy butter ingredients in a bowl.
2. Stir in steak cubes and mix well.
3. Cover and marinate in the refrigerator for 1 hour.
4. Divide the steak cubes in the air fryer baskets then use cooking spray.
5. Return the air fryer basket 1 to Zone 1, and basket 2 to Zone 2 of the Ninja Foodi 2-Basket Air Fryer.
6. Choose the "Air Fry" mode for Zone 1 at 400 degrees F and 15 minutes of cooking time.
7. Select the "MATCH COOK" option to copy the settings for Zone 2.
8. Initiate cooking by pressing the START/PAUSE BUTTON.
9. Serve warm.

Nutrition Info:

- (Per serving) Calories 264 | Fat 17g |Sodium 129mg | Carbs 0.9g | Fiber 0.3g | Sugar 0g | Protein 27g

Pork Chops With Broccoli

Servings: 2
Cooking Time: 13 Minutes.
Ingredients:

- 2 (5 ounces) bone-in pork chops
- 2 tablespoons avocado oil
- ½ teaspoon paprika
- ½ teaspoon onion powder
-
- ½ teaspoon garlic powder
- 1 teaspoon salt
- 2 cups broccoli florets
- 2 garlic cloves, minced

Directions:

1. Rub the pork chops with avocado oil, garlic, paprika, and spices.
2. Add pork chop to the crisper plate of Zone 1 in the Ninja Foodi Dual Zone Air Fryer.
3. Return the crisper plate to the Air Fryer.
4. Choose the Air Fry mode for Zone 1 and set the temperature to 400 degrees F and the time to 12 minutes.
5. Add the broccoli to the Zone 2 drawer and return it to the unit.
6. Choose the Air Fry mode for Zone 2 with 375 degrees F and the time to 13 minutes.
7. Press the SYNC button to sync the finish time for both Zones.
8. Initiate cooking by pressing the START/STOP button.
9. Flip the pork once cooked halfway through.
10. Cut the hardened butter into the cubes and place them on top of the pork chops.
11. Serve warm with crispy broccoli florets

Nutrition Info:

- (Per serving) Calories 410 | Fat 17.8g |Sodium 619mg | Carbs 21g | Fiber 1.4g | Sugar 1.8g | Protein 38.4g

Balsamic Steak Tips With Roasted Asparagus And Mushroom Medley

Servings:4
Cooking Time: 25 Minutes

Ingredients:

- FOR THE STEAK TIPS
- 1½ pounds sirloin tips
- ½ cup olive oil
- ¼ cup balsamic vinegar
- ¼ cup packed light brown sugar
- 1 tablespoon reduced-sodium soy sauce
- 1 teaspoon finely chopped fresh rosemary
-
- 1 teaspoon minced garlic
- FOR THE ASPARAGUS AND MUSHROOMS
- 6 ounces sliced cremini mushrooms
- 1 small red onion, sliced
- 1 tablespoon olive oil
- 1 pound asparagus, tough ends trimmed
- ⅛ teaspoon kosher salt

Directions:

1. To prep the steak tips: In a large bowl, combine the sirloin tips, oil, vinegar, brown sugar, soy sauce, rosemary, and garlic. Mix well to coat the steak.
2. To prep the mushrooms: In a large bowl, combine the mushrooms, onion, and oil.
3. To cook the steak and vegetables: Install a crisper plate in each of the two baskets. Shake any excess marinade from the steak tips, place the steak in the Zone 1 basket, and insert the basket in the unit. Place the mushrooms and onions in the Zone 2 basket and insert the basket in the unit.
4. Select Zone 1, select AIR FRY, set the temperature to 400°F, and set the time to 12 minutes.
5. Select Zone 2, select ROAST, set the temperature to 400°F, and set the time to 25 minutes. Select SMART FINISH.
6. Press START/PAUSE to begin cooking.
7. When the Zone 2 timer reads 10 minutes, press START/PAUSE. Remove the basket, add the asparagus to the mushrooms and onion, and sprinkle with salt. Reinsert the basket and press START/PAUSE to resume cooking.
8. When cooking is complete, the beef should be cooked to your liking and the asparagus crisp-tender. Serve warm.

Nutrition Info:

- (Per serving) Calories: 524; Total fat: 33g; Saturated fat: 2.5g; Carbohydrates: 16g; Fiber: 3g; Protein: 41g; Sodium: 192mg

Tasty Pork Skewers

Servings: 3
Cooking Time: 10 Minutes

Ingredients:

- 450g pork shoulder, cut into ¼-inch pieces
- 66ml soy sauce
- ½ tbsp garlic, crushed
- 1 tbsp ginger paste
- 1 ½ tsp sesame oil
- 22ml rice vinegar
- 21ml honey
- Pepper
- Salt

Directions:

1. In a bowl, mix meat with the remaining ingredients. Cover and place in the refrigerator for 30 minutes.
2. Thread the marinated meat onto the soaked skewers.
3. Insert a crisper plate in the Ninja Foodi air fryer baskets.
4. Place the pork skewers in both baskets.
5. Select zone 1, then select "air fry" mode and set the temperature to 360 degrees F for 10 minutes. Press "match" and then press "start/stop" to begin. Turn halfway through.

Nutrition Info:

- (Per serving) Calories 520 | Fat 34.7g |Sodium 1507mg | Carbs 12.2g | Fiber 0.5g | Sugar 9.1g | Protein 37g

Jerk-rubbed Pork Loin With Carrots And Sage

Servings: 4
Cooking Time: 35 Minutes

Ingredients:

- 1½ pounds pork loin
- 3 teaspoons canola oil, divided
- 2 tablespoons jerk seasoning
- 1-pound carrots, peeled, cut into 1-inch pieces
-
- 1 tablespoon honey
- ½ teaspoon kosher salt
- ½ teaspoon chopped fresh sage

Directions:

1. Place the pork loin in a pan or a dish with a high wall. Using a paper towel, pat the meat dry.
2. Rub 2 teaspoons of canola oil evenly over the pork with your hands. Then spread the jerk seasoning evenly over it with your hands.
3. Allow the pork loin to marinate for at least 10 minutes or up to 8 hours in the refrigerator after wrapping it in plastic wrap or sealing it in a plastic bag.
4. Toss the carrots with the remaining canola oil and ½ teaspoon of salt in a medium mixing bowl.
5. Place a crisper plate in each of the drawers. Put the marinated pork loin in the zone 1 drawer and place it in the unit. Place the carrots in the zone 2 drawer and place the drawer in the unit.
6. Select zone 1 and select AIR FRY. Set the temperature to 390 degrees F/ 200 degrees C and the time setting to 25 minutes. Select zone 2 and select AIR FRY. Set the temperature to 390 degrees F/ 200 degrees C and the time setting to 16 minutes. Select SYNC. Press START/STOP to begin cooking.
7. Check the pork loin for doneness after the zones have finished cooking. When the internal temperature of the loin hits 145°F on an instant-read thermometer, the pork is ready.
8. Allow the pork loin to rest for at least 5 minutes on a plate or cutting board.
9. Combine the carrots and sage in a mixing bowl.
10. When the pork loin has rested, slice it into the desired thickness of slices and serve with the carrots.

Nutrition Info:

- (Per serving) Calories 500 | Fat 19.8g | Sodium 680mg | Carbs 50.1g | Fiber 4.1g | Sugar 0g | Protein 27.9g

Italian Sausages With Peppers, Potatoes, And Onions

Servings:4
Cooking Time: 22 Minutes

Ingredients:

- FOR THE PEPPERS, POTATOES, AND ONIONS
- 2 Yukon Gold potatoes, cut into ¼-inch slices
- 1 red bell pepper, sliced
- 1 yellow onion, sliced
- ¼ cup canned tomato sauce
- 1 tablespoon olive oil
-
- 1 teaspoon minced garlic
- ½ teaspoon dried oregano
- ¼ teaspoon kosher salt
- FOR THE SAUSAGES
- 4 links Italian sausage

Directions:

1. To prep the peppers, potatoes, and onions: In a large bowl, combine the potatoes, pepper, onion, tomato sauce, oil, garlic, oregano, and salt. Mix to combine.
2. To cook the sausage and vegetables: Install a crisper plate in each of the two baskets. Place the sausages in the Zone 1 basket and insert the basket in the unit. Place the potato mixture in the Zone 2 basket and insert the basket in the unit.
3. Select Zone 1, select AIR FRY, set the temperature to 390°F, and set the time to 22 minutes.
4. Select Zone 2, select ROAST, set the temperature to 375°F, and set the time to 20 minutes. Select SMART FINISH.
5. Press START/PAUSE to begin cooking.
6. When cooking is complete, the sausages will be cooked through and the vegetables tender.
7. Slice the sausages into rounds, then mix them into the potato and pepper mixture. Serve.

Nutrition Info:

- (Per serving) Calories: 335; Total fat: 22g; Saturated fat: 6.5g; Carbohydrates: 21g; Fiber: 2g; Protein: 15g; Sodium: 658mg

Barbecue Ribs With Roasted Green Beans And Shallots

Servings:4
Cooking Time: 40 Minutes
Ingredients:

- FOR THE RIBS
- 1 tablespoon light brown sugar
- 1 tablespoon smoked paprika
- 1 tablespoon chili powder
- 2 teaspoons kosher salt
- 1 teaspoon freshly ground black pepper
- 1 teaspoon garlic powder
- ¼ teaspoon cayenne pepper (optional)
- 2 pounds pork ribs
- 1 cup barbecue sauce (your favorite), for serving
- FOR THE GREEN BEANS AND SHALLOTS
- 1 pound green beans, trimmed
- 2 shallots, sliced
- 1 tablespoon olive oil
- ¼ teaspoon kosher salt

Directions:

1. To prep the ribs: In a small bowl, combine the brown sugar, paprika, chili powder, salt, black pepper, garlic powder, and cayenne (if using).
2. Rub the spice blend all over both sides of the ribs.
3. To prep the green beans and shallots: In a large bowl, combine the green beans, shallots, and oil. Toss to coat. Season with the salt.
4. To cook the ribs and vegetables: Install a crisper plate in each of the two baskets. Place the ribs in the Zone 1 basket and insert the basket in the unit. Place the green beans in the Zone 2 basket and insert the basket in the unit.
5. Select Zone 1, select AIR FRY, set the temperature to 375°F, and set the time to 40 minutes.
6. Select Zone 2, select ROAST, set the temperature to 400°F, and set the time to 20 minutes. Select SMART FINISH.
7. Press START/PAUSE to begin cooking.
8. When the Zone 1 timer reads 10 minutes, press START/PAUSE. Increase the temperature of Zone 1 to 400°F. Press START/PAUSE to resume cooking.
9. When cooking is complete, an instant-read thermometer inserted into the ribs should read 170°F and the green beans should be tender-crisp. Serve topped with your favorite barbecue sauce.

Nutrition Info:

- (Per serving) Calories: 541; Total fat: 27g; Saturated fat: 9g; Carbohydrates: 48g; Fiber: 4.5g; Protein: 28g; Sodium: 1,291mg

Beef & Broccoli

Servings:4
Cooking Time:12
Ingredients:

- 12 ounces of teriyaki sauce, divided
- ½ tablespoon garlic powder
- ¼ cup of soy sauce
- 1 pound raw sirloin steak, thinly sliced
- 2 cups broccoli, cut into florets
- 2 teaspoons of olive oil
- Salt and black pepper, to taste

Directions:

1. Take a zip-lock plastic bag and mix teriyaki sauce, salt, garlic powder, black pepper, soy sauce, and olive oil.
2. Marinate the beef in it for 2 hours.
3. Then drain the beef from the marinade.
4. Now toss the broccoli with oil, teriyaki sauce, and salt and black pepper.
5. Put it in a zone 1 basket
6. Now for the zone, 1 basket set it to AIRFRY mode at 400 degrees F for 15 minutes.
7. Place the steak in a zone 2 basket and set it to AIR FRY mode at 375 degrees F for 10-12 minutes.
8. Hit start and let the cooking cycle completes.
9. Once it's done take out the beef and broccoli and
10. serve immediately with leftover teriyaki sauce and cooked rice.

Nutrition Info:

- (Per serving) Calories 344| Fat 10g| Sodium 4285mg | Carbs18.2 g | Fiber 1.5g| Sugar 13.3g | Protein42 g

Lamb Chops With Dijon Garlic

Servings: 4
Cooking Time: 22 Minutes
Ingredients:

- 2 teaspoons Dijon mustard
- 2 teaspoons olive oil
- 1 teaspoon soy sauce
- 1 teaspoon garlic, minced
- 1 teaspoon cumin powder
-
- 1 teaspoon cayenne pepper
- 1 teaspoon Italian spice blend (optional)
- ¼ teaspoon salt
- 8 lamb chops

Directions:

1. Combine the Dijon mustard, olive oil, soy sauce, garlic, cumin powder, cayenne pepper, Italian spice blend (optional), and salt in a medium mixing bowl.
2. Put the marinade in a large Ziploc bag. Add the lamb chops. Seal the bag tightly after pressing out the air. Coat the lamb in the marinade by shaking the bag and pressing the chops into the mixture. Place in the fridge for at least 30 minutes, or up to overnight, to marinate.
3. Install a crisper plate in both drawers. Place half the lamb chops in the zone 1 drawer and half in zone 2's, then insert the drawers into the unit.
4. Select zone 1, select AIR FRY, set temperature to 390 degrees F/ 200 degrees C, and set time to 22 minutes. Select MATCH to match zone 2 settings to zone 1. Press the START/STOP button to begin cooking.
5. When the time reaches 11 minutes, press START/STOP to pause the unit. Remove the drawers and flip the lamb chops. Re-insert the drawers into the unit and press START/STOP to resume cooking.
6. Serve and enjoy!

Nutrition Info:

- (Per serving) Calories 343 | Fat 15.1g | Sodium 380mg | Carbs 0.9 g | Fiber 0.3g | Sugar 0.1g | Protein 48.9g

Garlic-rosemary Pork Loin With Scalloped Potatoes And Cauliflower

Servings:6
Cooking Time: 50 Minutes

Ingredients:

- FOR THE PORK LOIN
- 2 pounds pork loin roast
- 2 tablespoons vegetable oil
- 2 teaspoons dried thyme
- 2 teaspoons dried crushed rosemary
- 1 teaspoon minced garlic
- ¾ teaspoon kosher salt
- FOR THE SCALLOPED POTATOES AND CAULIFLOWER
- 1 teaspoon vegetable oil
- ¾ pound Yukon Gold potatoes, peeled and very thinly sliced
- 1½ cups cauliflower florets
- ¼ teaspoon kosher salt
- ¼ teaspoon freshly ground black pepper
- 1 tablespoon very cold unsalted butter, grated
- 3 tablespoons all-purpose flour
- 1 cup whole milk
- 1 cup shredded Gruyère cheese

Directions:

1. To prep the pork loin: Coat the pork with the oil. Season with thyme, rosemary, garlic, and salt.
2. To prep the potatoes and cauliflower: Brush the bottom and sides of the Zone 2 basket with the oil. Add one-third of the potatoes to the bottom of the basket and arrange in a single layer. Top with ½ cup of cauliflower florets. Sprinkle a third of the salt and black pepper on top. Scatter one-third of the butter on top and sprinkle on 1 tablespoon of flour. Repeat this step twice more for a total of three layers.
3. Pour the milk over the layered potatoes and cauliflower; it should just cover the top layer. Top with the Gruyère.
4. To cook the pork and scalloped vegetables: Install a crisper plate in the Zone 1 basket. Place the pork loin in the basket and insert the basket in the unit. Insert the Zone 2 basket in the unit.
5. Select Zone 1, select AIR FRY, set the temperature to 390°F, and set the time to 50 minutes.
6. Select Zone 2, select BAKE, set the temperature to 350°F, and set the time to 45 minutes. Select SMART FINISH.
7. Press START/PAUSE to begin cooking.
8. When cooking is complete, the pork will be cooked through (an instant-read thermometer should read 145°F) and the potatoes and cauliflower will be tender.
9. Let the pork rest for at least 15 minutes before slicing and serving with the scalloped vegetables.

Nutrition Info:

- (Per serving) Calories: 439; Total fat: 25g; Saturated fat: 10g; Carbohydrates: 17g; Fiber: 1.5g; Protein: 37g; Sodium: 431mg

Mongolian Beef With Sweet Chili Brussels Sprouts

Servings:4
Cooking Time: 20 Minutes

Ingredients:

- FOR THE MONGOLIAN BEEF
- 1 pound flank steak, cut into thin strips
- 1 tablespoon olive oil
- 2 tablespoons cornstarch
- ½ cup reduced-sodium soy sauce
- ½ cup packed light brown sugar
- 1 tablespoon chili paste (optional)
- 1 tablespoon minced garlic
- 1 tablespoon minced fresh ginger
- 2 scallions, chopped
- FOR THE BRUSSELS SPROUTS
- 1 pound Brussels sprouts, halved lengthwise
- 1 tablespoon olive oil
- ½ cup gochujang sauce
- 2 tablespoons rice vinegar
- 1 tablespoon reduced-sodium soy sauce
- 1 tablespoon light brown sugar
- 1 teaspoon fresh garlic

Directions:

1. To prep the Mongolian beef: In a large bowl, combine the flank steak and olive oil and toss to coat. Add the cornstarch and toss to coat.
2. In a small bowl, whisk together the soy sauce, brown sugar, chili paste (if using), garlic, and ginger. Set the soy sauce mixture aside.
3. To prep the Brussels sprouts: In a large bowl, combine the Brussels sprouts and oil and toss to coat.
4. In a small bowl, whisk together the gochujang sauce, vinegar, soy sauce, brown sugar, and garlic. Set the chili sauce mixture aside.
5. To cook the beef and Brussels sprouts: Install a crisper plate in each of the two baskets. Place the beef in the Zone 1 basket and insert the basket in the unit. Place the Brussels sprouts in the Zone 2 basket and insert the basket in the unit.
6. Select Zone 1, select AIR FRY, set the temperature to 390°F, and set the time to 15 minutes.
7. Select Zone 2, select AIR FRY, set the temperature to 400°F, and set the time to 20 minutes. Select SMART FINISH.
8. Press START/PAUSE to begin cooking.
9. When both timers read 5 minutes, press START/PAUSE. Remove the Zone 1 basket, add the reserved soy sauce mixture and the scallions, and toss with the beef. Reinsert the basket. Remove the Zone 2 basket, add the reserved chili sauce mixture, and toss with the Brussels sprouts. Reinsert the basket and press START/PAUSE to resume cooking.
10. When cooking is complete, the steak should be cooked through and the Brussels sprouts tender and slightly caramelized. Serve warm.

Nutrition Info:

- (Per serving) Calories: 481; Total fat: 16g; Saturated fat: 4.5g; Carbohydrates: 60g; Fiber: 5g; Protein: 27g; Sodium: 2,044mg

Pork Katsu With Seasoned Rice

Servings:4
Cooking Time: 15 Minutes

Ingredients:

- FOR THE PORK KATSU
- 4 thin-sliced boneless pork chops (4 ounces each)
- 2 tablespoons all-purpose flour
- 2 large eggs
- 1 cup panko bread crumbs
- ¼ teaspoon kosher salt
- ¼ teaspoon freshly ground black pepper
- 1 teaspoon vegetable oil
- 3 tablespoons ketchup
- 3 tablespoons Worcestershire sauce
- 1 tablespoon oyster sauce
- ⅛ teaspoon granulated sugar
- FOR THE RICE
- 2 cups dried instant rice (not microwavable)
- 2½ cups water
- 1 tablespoon sesame oil
- 1 teaspoon soy sauce
- 1 tablespoon toasted sesame seeds
- 3 scallions, sliced

Directions:

1. To prep the pork katsu: Place the pork chops between two slices of plastic wrap. Using a meat mallet or rolling pin, pound the pork into ½-inch-thick cutlets.
2. Set up a breading station with three small shallow bowls. Place the flour in the first bowl. In the second bowl, whisk the eggs. Combine the panko, salt, and black pepper in the third bowl.
3. Bread the cutlets in this order: First, dip them in the flour, coating both sides. Then, dip them into the beaten egg. Finally, coat them in panko, gently pressing the bread crumbs to adhere to the pork. Drizzle both sides of the cutlets with the oil.
4. To prep the rice: In the Zone 2 basket, combine the rice, water, sesame oil, and soy sauce. Stir well to ensure all of the rice is submerged in the liquid.
5. To cook the pork and rice: Install a crisper plate in the Zone 1 basket. Place the pork in the basket and insert the basket in the unit. Insert the Zone 2 basket in the unit.
6. Select Zone 1, select AIR FRY, set the temperature to 390°F, and set the time to 15 minutes.
7. Select Zone 2, select BAKE, set the temperature to 350°F, and set the time to 10 minutes. Select SMART FINISH.
8. Press START/PAUSE to begin cooking.
9. When the Zone 1 timer reads 10 minutes, press START/PAUSE. Remove the basket and use silicone-tipped tongs to flip the pork. Reinsert the basket and press START/PAUSE to resume cooking.
10. When cooking is complete, the pork should be crisp and cooked through and the rice tender.
11. Stir the sesame seeds and scallions into the rice. For the sauce to go with the pork, in a small bowl, whisk together the ketchup, Worcestershire sauce, oyster sauce, and sugar. Drizzle the sauce over the pork and serve with the hot rice.

Nutrition Info:

- (Per serving) Calories: 563; Total fat: 20g; Saturated fat: 5.5g; Carbohydrates: 62g; Fiber: 1g; Protein: 34g; Sodium: 665mg

Steak And Mashed Creamy Potatoes

Servings:1
Cooking Time:45

Ingredients:

- 2 Russet potatoes, peeled and cubed
- ¼ cup butter, divided
- 1/3 cup heavy cream
- ½ cup shredded cheddar cheese
- Salt and black pepper, to taste
- 1 New York strip steak, about a pound
- 1 teaspoon of olive oil
- Oil spray, for greasing

Directions:

1. Rub the potatoes with salt and a little amount of olive oil about a teaspoon.
2. Next, season the steak with salt and black pepper.
3. Place the russet potatoes in a zone 1 basket.
4. Oil spray the steak from both sides and then place it in the zone 2 basket.
5. Set zone 1 to AIR fry mode for 45 minutes at 390 degrees F.
6. Set the zone 2 basket, at 12 minutes at 375 degrees F.
7. Hot start and Lethe ninja foodie do its magic.
8. One the cooking cycle completes, take out the steak and potatoes.
9. Mash the potatoes and then add butter, heavy cream, and cheese along with salt and black pepper.
10. Serve the mashed potatoes with steak.
11. Enjoy.

Nutrition Info:

- (Per serving) Calories1932 | Fat 85.2g| Sodium 3069mg | Carbs 82g | Fiber10.3 g| Sugar 5.3g | Protein 22.5g

Air Fried Lamb Chops

Servings: 4
Cooking Time: 10 Minutes

Ingredients:

- 700g lamb chops
- ½ teaspoon oregano
- 3 tablespoons parsley, minced
- ½ teaspoon black pepper
- 3 cloves garlic minced
- 2 tablespoons lemon juice
- 2 tablespoons olive oil
- Salt to taste

Directions:

1. Pat dry the chops and mix with lemon juice and the rest of the ingredients.
2. Place these chops in the air fryer baskets.
3. Return the air fryer basket 1 to Zone 1, and basket 2 to Zone 2 of the Ninja Foodi 2-Basket Air Fryer.
4. Choose the "Air Fry" mode for Zone 1and set the temperature to 400 degrees F and 10 minutes of cooking time.
5. Select the "MATCH COOK" option to copy the settings for Zone 2.
6. Initiate cooking by pressing the START/PAUSE BUTTON.
7. Flip the pork chops once cooked halfway through.
8. Serve warm.

Nutrition Info:

- (Per serving) Calories 396 | Fat 23.2g |Sodium 622mg | Carbs 0.7g | Fiber 0g | Sugar 0g | Protein 45.6g

Steak And Asparagus Bundles

Servings: 6
Cooking Time: 10 Minutes

Ingredients:

- 907g flank steak, cut into 6 pieces
- Salt and black pepper, to taste
- ½ cup tamari sauce
- 2 cloves garlic, crushed
- 455g asparagus, trimmed
- 3 capsicums, sliced
- ¼ cup balsamic vinegar
- 79 ml beef broth
- 2 tablespoons unsalted butter
- Olive oil spray

Directions:

1. Mix steaks with black pepper, tamari sauce, and garlic in a Ziplock bag.
2. Seal the bag, shake well and refrigerate for 1 hour.
3. Place the steaks on the working surface and top each with asparagus and capsicums.
4. Roll the steaks and secure them with toothpicks.
5. Place these rolls in the air fryer baskets.
6. Return the air fryer basket 1 to Zone 1, and basket 2 to Zone 2 of the Ninja Foodi 2-Basket Air Fryer.
7. Choose the "Air Fry" mode for Zone 1 and set the temperature to 400 degrees F and 10 minutes of cooking time.
8. Select the "MATCH COOK" option to copy the settings for Zone 2.
9. Initiate cooking by pressing the START/PAUSE BUTTON.
10. Meanwhile, cook broth with butter and vinegar in a saucepan.
11. Cook this mixture until reduced by half and adjust seasoning with black pepper and salt.
12. Serve the steak rolls with the prepared sauce.

Nutrition Info:

- (Per serving) Calories 551 | Fat 31g |Sodium 1329mg | Carbs 1½g | Fiber 0.8g | Sugar 0.4g | Protein 64g

Juicy Pork Chops

Servings: 4
Cooking Time: 15 Minutes

Ingredients:

- 450g pork chops
- ¼ tsp garlic powder
- 15ml olive oil
- ¼ tsp smoked paprika
- Pepper
- Salt

Directions:

1. In a small bowl, mix the garlic powder, paprika, pepper, and salt.
2. Brush the pork chops with oil and rub with spice mixture.
3. Insert a crisper plate in the Ninja Foodi air fryer baskets.
4. Place the pork chops in both baskets.
5. Select zone 1, then select "bake" mode and set the temperature to 410 degrees F for 15 minutes. Press "match" to match zone 2 settings to zone 1. Press "start/stop" to begin. Turn halfway through.

Nutrition Info:

- (Per serving) Calories 394 | Fat 31.7g |Sodium 118mg | Carbs 0.2g | Fiber 0.1g | Sugar 0.1g | Protein 25.5g

Air Fryer Meatloaves

Servings: 4
Cooking Time: 22 Minutes.

Ingredients:

- ⅓ cup milk
- 2 tablespoons basil pesto
- 1 egg, beaten
- 1 garlic clove, minced
- ¼ teaspoons black pepper
-
- 1 lb. ground beef
- ⅓ cup panko bread crumbs
- 8 pepperoni slices
- ½ cup marinara sauce, warmed
- 1 tablespoon fresh basil, chopped

Directions:

1. Mix pesto, milk, egg, garlic, and black pepper in a medium-sized bowl.
2. Stir in ground beef and bread crumbs, then mix.
3. Make the 4 small-sized loaves with this mixture and top them with 2 pepperoni slices.
4. Press the slices into the meatloaves.
5. Place the meatloaves in the two crisper plates.
6. Return the crisper plate to the Ninja Foodi Dual Zone Air Fryer.
7. Choose the Air Fry mode for Zone 1 and set the temperature to 390 degrees F and the time to 22 minutes.
8. Select the "MATCH" button to copy the settings for Zone 2.
9. Initiate cooking by pressing the START/STOP button.
10. Top them with marinara sauce and basil to serve.
11. Serve warm.

Nutrition Info:

- (Per serving) Calories 316 | Fat 12.2g |Sodium 587mg | Carbs 12.2g | Fiber 1g | Sugar 1.8g | Protein 25.8g

Chipotle Beef

Servings: 4
Cooking Time: 18 Minutes.

Ingredients:

- 1 lb. beef steak, cut into chunks
- 1 large egg
- ½ cup parmesan cheese, grated
- ½ cup pork panko
- ½ teaspoon seasoned salt
- Chipotle Ranch Dip
-
- ¼ cup mayonnaise
- ¼ cup sour cream
- 1 teaspoon chipotle paste
- ½ teaspoon ranch dressing mix
- ¼ medium lime, juiced

Directions:

1. Mix all the ingredients for chipotle ranch dip in a bowl.
2. Keep it in the refrigerator for 30 minutes.
3. Mix pork panko with salt and parmesan.
4. Beat egg in one bowl and spread the panko mixture in another flat bowl.
5. Dip the steak chunks in the egg first, then coat them with panko mixture.
6. Spread them in the two crisper plates and spray them with cooking oil.
7. Return the crisper plate to the Ninja Foodi Dual Zone Air Fryer.
8. Choose the Air Fry mode for Zone 1 and set the temperature to 390 degrees F and the time to 18 minutes.
9. Select the "MATCH" button to copy the settings for Zone 2.
10. Initiate cooking by pressing the START/STOP button.
11. Serve with chipotle ranch and salt and pepper on top. Enjoy.

Nutrition Info:

- (Per serving) Calories 310 | Fat 17g |Sodium 271mg | Carbs 4.3g | Fiber 0.9g | Sugar 2.1g | Protein 35g

Chapter 5 Poultry Recipes

Chicken Parmesan With Roasted Lemon-parmesan Broccoli

Servings:4
Cooking Time: 18 Minutes

Ingredients:

- FOR THE CHICKEN PARMESAN
- 2 tablespoons all-purpose flour
- 2 large eggs
- 1 cup panko bread crumbs
- 2 tablespoons grated Parmesan cheese
- 2 teaspoons Italian seasoning
- 4 thin-sliced chicken cutlets (4 ounces each)
- 2 tablespoons vegetable oil
- ½ cup marinara sauce
- ½ cup shredded part-skim mozzarella cheese
- FOR THE BROCCOLI
- 4 cups broccoli florets
- 2 tablespoons olive oil, divided
- ¼ teaspoon kosher salt
- ¼ teaspoon freshly ground black pepper
- 2 teaspoons fresh lemon juice
- 2 tablespoons grated Parmesan cheese

Directions:

1. To prep the chicken Parmesan: Set up a breading station with 3 small shallow bowls. Place the flour in the first bowl. In the second bowl, beat the eggs. Combine the panko, Parmesan, and Italian seasoning in the third bowl.
2. Bread the chicken cutlets in this order: First, dip them into the flour, coating both sides. Then, dip into the beaten egg. Finally, place in the panko mixture, coating both sides of the cutlets. Drizzle the oil over the cutlets.
3. To prep the broccoli: In a large bowl, combine the broccoli, 1 tablespoon of olive oil, the salt, and black pepper.
4. To cook the chicken and broccoli: Install a crisper plate in the Zone 1 basket. Place the chicken in the basket and insert the basket in the unit. Place the broccoli in the Zone 2 basket and insert the basket in the unit.
5. Select Zone 1, select AIR FRY, set the temperature to 390°F, and set the time to 18 minutes.
6. Select Zone 2, select ROAST, set the temperature to 390°F, and set the time to 15 minutes. Select SMART FINISH.
7. Press START/PAUSE to begin cooking.
8. When the Zone 1 timer reads 10 minutes, press START/PAUSE. Remove the basket and use silicone-tipped tongs to flip the chicken. Reinsert the basket and press START/PAUSE to resume cooking.
9. When the Zone 1 timer reads 2 minutes, press START/PAUSE. Remove the basket and spoon 2 tablespoons of marinara sauce over each chicken cutlet. Sprinkle the mozzarella on top. Reinsert the basket and press START/PAUSE to resume cooking.
10. When cooking is complete, the cheese will be melted and the chicken cooked through (an instant-read thermometer should read 165°F). Transfer the broccoli to a large bowl. Add the lemon juice and Parmesan and toss to coat. Serve the chicken and broccoli warm.

Nutrition Info:

- (Per serving) Calories: 462; Total fat: 22g; Saturated fat: 5g; Carbohydrates: 25g; Fiber: 2.5g; Protein: 37g; Sodium: 838mg

Chicken Drumettes

Servings: 5
Cooking Time: 52 Minutes.

Ingredients:

- 10 large chicken drumettes
- Cooking spray
- ¼ cup of rice vinegar
- 3 tablespoons honey
- 2 tablespoons unsalted chicken stock
- 1 tablespoon soy sauce
- 1 tablespoon toasted sesame oil
- ⅜ teaspoons crushed red pepper
- 1 garlic clove, chopped
- 2 tablespoons chopped unsalted roasted peanuts
- 1 tablespoon chopped fresh chives

Directions:

1. Spread the chicken in the two crisper plates in an even layer and spray cooking spray on top.
2. Return the crisper plate to the Ninja Foodi Dual Zone Air Fryer.
3. Choose the Air Fry mode for Zone 1 and set the temperature to 390 degrees F and the time to 47 minutes.
4. Select the "MATCH" button to copy the settings for Zone 2.
5. Initiate cooking by pressing the START/STOP button.
6. Flip the chicken drumettes once cooked halfway through, then resume cooking.
7. During this time, mix soy sauce, honey, stock, vinegar, garlic, and crushed red pepper in a suitable saucepan and place it over medium-high heat to cook on a simmer.
8. Cook this sauce for 6 minutes with occasional stirring, then pour it into a medium-sized bowl.
9. Add air fried drumettes and toss well to coat with the honey sauce.
10. Garnish with chives and peanuts.
11. Serve warm and fresh.

Nutrition Info:

- (Per serving) Calories 268 | Fat 10.4g |Sodium 411mg | Carbs 0.4g | Fiber 0.1g | Sugar 0.1g | Protein 40.6g

Cornish Hen

Servings: 4
Cooking Time: 35 Minutes

Ingredients:

- 2 Cornish hens
- 2 tablespoons olive oil
- 2 teaspoons salt
- 1½ teaspoons Italian seasoning
-
- 1 teaspoon garlic powder
- 1 teaspoon paprika
- ½ teaspoon black pepper
- ½ teaspoon lemon zest

Directions:

1. Mix Italian seasoning with lemon zest, juice, black pepper, paprika, and garlic powder in a bowl.
2. Rub each hen with the seasoning mixture.
3. Tuck the hen wings in and place one in each air fryer basket.
4. Return the air fryer basket 1 to Zone 1, and basket 2 to Zone 2 of the Ninja Foodi 2-Basket Air Fryer.
5. Choose the "Air Fry" mode for Zone 1 and set the temperature to 375 degrees F and 35 minutes of cooking time.
6. Select the "MATCH COOK" option to copy the settings for Zone 2.
7. Initiate cooking by pressing the START/PAUSE BUTTON.
8. Flip the hens once cooked halfway through.
9. Serve warm.

Nutrition Info:

- (Per serving) Calories 223 | Fat 11.7g |Sodium 721mg | Carbs 13.6g | Fiber 0.7g | Sugar 8g | Protein 15.7g

Crispy Sesame Chicken

Servings: 2
Cooking Time: 10 Minutes

Ingredients:

- 680g boneless chicken thighs, diced
- 2 tablespoons rice vinegar
- 1 tablespoon soy sauce
- 2 teaspoons minced fresh ginger
- 1 garlic clove, minced
- ¾ teaspoon salt
- ½ teaspoon black pepper
- 2 large eggs, beaten
- 1 cup cornstarch
- Sauce
- 59ml soy sauce
-
- 2 tablespoons rice vinegar
- ⅓ cup brown sugar
- 59ml water
- 1 tablespoon cornstarch
- 2 teaspoons sesame oil
- 2 tablespoons vegetable oil
- 2 garlic cloves, minced
- 2 teaspoons chile paste
- Garnish
- 1 tablespoon toasted sesame seeds

Directions:

1. Blend all the sauce ingredients in a saucepan and cook until it thickens then allow it to cool.
2. Mix chicken with black pepper, salt, garlic, ginger, vinegar, and soy sauce in a bowl.
3. Cover and marinate the chicken for 20 minutes.
4. Divide the chicken in the air fryer baskets.
5. Return the air fryer basket 1 to Zone 1, and basket 2 to Zone 2 of the Ninja Foodi 2-Basket Air Fryer.
6. Choose the "Air Fry" mode for Zone 1 and set the temperature to 400 degrees F and 10 minutes of cooking time.
7. Select the "MATCH COOK" option to copy the settings for Zone 2.
8. Initiate cooking by pressing the START/PAUSE BUTTON.
9. Pour the prepared sauce over the air fried chicken and drizzle sesame seeds on top.
10. Serve warm.

Nutrition Info:

- (Per serving) Calories 351 | Fat 16g |Sodium 777mg | Carbs 26g | Fiber 4g | Sugar 5g | Protein 28g

Air Fried Chicken Legs

Servings: 4
Cooking Time: 10 Minutes

Ingredients:

- 8 chicken legs
- 2 tablespoons olive oil
- 1 teaspoon salt
- 1 teaspoon black pepper
- 1 teaspoon smoked paprika
- 1 teaspoon garlic powder
- 1 teaspoon dried parsley

Directions:

1. Mix chicken with oil, herbs and spices in a bowl.
2. Divide the chicken legs in the air fryer baskets.
3. Return the air fryer basket 1 to Zone 1, and basket 2 to Zone 2 of the Ninja Foodi 2-Basket Air Fryer.
4. Choose the "Air Fry" mode for Zone 1 at 400 degrees F and 10 minutes of cooking time.
5. Select the "MATCH COOK" option to copy the settings for Zone 2.
6. Initiate cooking by pressing the START/PAUSE BUTTON.
7. Flip the chicken once cooked halfway through.
8. Serve warm.

Nutrition Info:

- (Per serving) Calories 220 | Fat 13g |Sodium 542mg | Carbs 0.9g | Fiber 0.3g | Sugar 0.2g | Protein 25.6g

Chicken And Potatoes

Servings: 2
Cooking Time: 10 Minutes
Ingredients:

- 2 potatoes, diced
- 2 chicken breasts, diced
- 4 cloves garlic crushed
- 2 teaspoons smoked paprika
- ½ teaspoon red chili flakes
- 1 teaspoon fresh thyme
- 1 teaspoon salt
- ¼ teaspoon black pepper
- 2 tablespoons olive oil

Directions:

1. Rub chicken with half of the salt, black pepper, oil, thyme, red chili flakes, paprika and garlic.
2. Mix potatoes with remaining spices, oil and garlic in a bowl.
3. Add chicken to one air fryer basket and potatoes the second basket.
4. Return the air fryer basket 1 to Zone 1, and basket 2 to Zone 2 of the Ninja Foodi 2-Basket Air Fryer.
5. Choose the "Air Fry" mode for Zone 1 at 375 degrees F and 10 minutes of cooking time.
6. Select the "MATCH COOK" option to copy the settings for Zone 2.
7. Initiate cooking by pressing the START/PAUSE BUTTON.
8. Flip the chicken and toss potatoes once cooked halfway through.
9. Garnish with chopped parsley.
10. Serve chicken with the potatoes.

Nutrition Info:

- (Per serving) Calories 374 | Fat 13g |Sodium 552mg | Carbs 25g | Fiber 1.2g | Sugar 1.2g | Protein 37.7g

Chicken Caprese

Servings: 4
Cooking Time: 10 Minutes
Ingredients:

- 4 chicken breast cutlets
- 1 teaspoon Italian seasoning
- 1 teaspoon salt
- ½ teaspoon black pepper
- 4 slices fresh mozzarella cheese
- 1 large tomato, sliced
- Basil and balsamic vinegar to garnish

Directions:

1. Pat dry the chicken cutlets with a kitchen towel.
2. Rub the chicken with Italian seasoning, black pepper and salt.
3. Place two chicken breasts in each air fryer basket.
4. Return the air fryer basket 1 to Zone 1, and basket 2 to Zone 2 of the Ninja Foodi 2-Basket Air Fryer.
5. Choose the "Air Fry" mode for Zone 1 at 375 degrees F and 10 minutes of cooking time.
6. Select the "MATCH COOK" option to copy the settings for Zone 2.
7. Initiate cooking by pressing the START/PAUSE BUTTON.
8. After 10 minutes top each chicken breast with a slice of cheese and tomato slices.
9. Return the baskets to the Ninja Foodi 2 Baskets Air Fryer and air fry for 5 another minutes.
10. Garnish with balsamic vinegar and basil.
11. Serve warm.

Nutrition Info:

- (Per serving) Calories 502 | Fat 25g |Sodium 230mg | Carbs 1.5g | Fiber 0.2g | Sugar 0.4g | Protein 64.1g

Coconut Chicken Tenders With Broiled Utica Greens

Servings:4

Cooking Time: 25 Minutes

Ingredients:

- FOR THE CHICKEN TENDERS
- 2 tablespoons all-purpose flour
- 2 large eggs
- 1 cup unsweetened shredded coconut
- ¾ cup panko bread crumbs
- ½ teaspoon kosher salt
- 1½ pounds chicken tenders
- Nonstick cooking spray
- FOR THE UTICA GREENS
- 12 ounces frozen chopped escarole or Swiss chard, thawed and drained
- ¼ cup diced prosciutto
- 2 tablespoons chopped pickled cherry peppers
- ½ teaspoon garlic powder
- ½ teaspoon onion powder
- ¼ teaspoon kosher salt
- ¼ cup Italian-style bread crumbs
- ¼ cup grated Romano cheese
- Nonstick cooking spray

Directions:

1. To prep the chicken tenders: Set up a breading station with three small shallow bowls. Place the flour in the first bowl. In the second bowl, beat the eggs. Combine the coconut, bread crumbs, and salt in the third bowl.
2. Bread the chicken tenders in this order: First, coat them in the flour. Then, dip into the beaten egg. Finally, coat them in the coconut breading, gently pressing the breading into the chicken to help it adhere. Mist both sides of each tender with cooking spray.
3. To prep the Utica greens: In the Zone 2 basket, mix the greens, prosciutto, cherry peppers, garlic powder, onion powder, and salt. Scatter the bread crumbs and Romano cheese over the top. Spritz the greens with cooking spray.
4. To cook the chicken and greens: Install a crisper plate in the Zone 1 basket. Place the chicken tenders in the basket in a single layer and insert the basket in the unit. Insert the Zone 2 basket in the unit.
5. Select Zone 1, select AIR FRY, set the temperature to 390°F, and set the time to 25 minutes.
6. Select Zone 2, select AIR BROIL, set the temperature to 450°F, and set the time to 10 minutes. Select SMART FINISH.
7. Press START/PAUSE to begin cooking.
8. When cooking is complete, the chicken will be crispy and cooked through (an instant-read thermometer should read 165°F) and the greens should be warmed through and toasted on top. Serve warm.

Nutrition Info:

- (Per serving) Calories: 527; Total fat: 26g; Saturated fat: 11g; Carbohydrates: 24g; Fiber: 6.5g; Protein: 50g; Sodium: 886mg

Chicken Drumsticks

Servings: 6
Cooking Time: 15 Minutes

Ingredients:

- 12 chicken drumsticks
- 72g chilli garlic sauce
- 2 tbsp ginger, minced
- 1 tbsp garlic, minced
- 3 green onion stalks, chopped
- 60ml orange juice
- 60ml soy sauce
- ½ medium onion, sliced
- Pepper
- Salt

Directions:

1. Add all the ingredients except the drumsticks into a blender and blend until smooth.
2. Place the chicken drumsticks in bowl.
3. Pour the blended mixture over chicken drumsticks and mix well.
4. Cover the bowl and place in refrigerator for 1 hour.
5. Insert a crisper plate in the Ninja Foodi air fryer baskets.
6. Place the marinated chicken drumsticks in both baskets.
7. Select zone 1 then select "air fry" mode and set the temperature to 390 degrees F for 15 minutes. Press "match" and then"start/stop" to begin.

Nutrition Info:

- (Per serving) Calories 178 | Fat 5.4g |Sodium 701mg | Carbs 4.5g | Fiber 0.6g | Sugar 1.5g | Protein 26.4g

Chicken & Veggies

Servings: 4
Cooking Time: 10 Minutes

Ingredients:

- 450g chicken breast, boneless & cut into pieces
- 2 garlic cloves, minced
- 15ml olive oil
- 239g frozen mix vegetables
- 1 tbsp Italian seasoning
- ½ tsp chilli powder
- ½ tsp garlic powder
- Pepper
- Salt

Directions:

1. In a bowl, toss chicken with remaining ingredients until well coated.
2. Insert a crisper plate in the Ninja Foodi air fryer baskets.
3. Add chicken and vegetables in both baskets.
4. Select zone 1 then select "air fry" mode and set the temperature to 390 degrees F for 10 minutes. Press "match" to match zone 2 settings to zone 1. Press "start/stop" to begin.

Nutrition Info:

- (Per serving) Calories 221 | Fat 7.6g |Sodium 126mg | Carbs 10.6g | Fiber 3.3g | Sugar 2.7g | Protein 26.3g

Spicy Chicken

Servings:40
Cooking Time:35
Ingredients:

- 4 chicken thighs
- 2 cups of butter milk
- 4 chicken legs
- 2 cups of flour
- Salt and black pepper, to taste
- 2 tablespoons garlic powder
- ½ teaspoon onion powder
- 1 teaspoon poultry seasoning
- 1 teaspoon cumin
- 2 tablespoons paprika
- 1 tablespoon olive oil

Directions:

1. Take a bowl and add buttermilk to it.
2. Soak the chicken thighs and chicken legs in the buttermilk for 2 hours.
3. Mix flour, all the seasonings, and olive oil in a small bowl.
4. Take out the chicken pieces from the buttermilk mixture and then dredge them into the flour mixture.
5. Repeat the steps for all the pieces and then arrange them into both the air fryer basket.
6. Set the timer for both the basket by selecting a roast mode for 35-40 minutes at 350 degrees F.
7. Once the cooking cycle complete select the pause button and then take out the basket.
8. Serve and enjoy.

Nutrition Info:

- (Per serving) Calories 624| Fat17.6 g| Sodium300 mg | Carbs 60g | Fiber 3.5g | Sugar 7.7g | Protein54.2 g

Greek Chicken Meatballs

Servings: 4
Cooking Time: 9 Minutes
Ingredients:

- 455g ground chicken
- 1 large egg
- 1½ tablespoons garlic paste
- 1 tablespoon dried oregano
- 1 teaspoon lemon zest
- 1 teaspoon dried onion powder
- ¾ teaspoon salt
- ¼ teaspoon black pepper
- Oil spray

Directions:

1. Mix ground chicken with rest of the ingredients in a bowl.
2. Make 1-inch sized meatballs out of this mixture.
3. Place the meatballs in the air fryer baskets.
4. Return the air fryer basket 1 to Zone 1, and basket 2 to Zone 2 of the Ninja Foodi 2-Basket Air Fryer.
5. Choose the "Air Fry" mode for Zone 1 and set the temperature to 390 degrees F and 9 minutes of cooking time.
6. Select the "MATCH COOK" option to copy the settings for Zone 2.
7. Initiate cooking by pressing the START/PAUSE BUTTON.
8. Serve warm.

Nutrition Info:

- (Per serving) Calories 346 | Fat 16.1g |Sodium 882mg | Carbs 1.3g | Fiber 0.5g | Sugar 0.5g | Protein 48.2g

Bang-bang Chicken

Servings: 2
Cooking Time: 20 Minutes.

Ingredients:

- 1 cup mayonnaise
- ½ cup sweet chili sauce
- 2 tablespoons Sriracha sauce
- ⅓ cup flour
-
- 1 lb. boneless chicken breast, diced
- 1 ½ cups panko bread crumbs
- 2 green onions, chopped

Directions:

1. Mix mayonnaise with Sriracha and sweet chili sauce in a large bowl.
2. Keep ¾ cup of the mixture aside.
3. Add flour, chicken, breadcrumbs, and remaining mayo mixture to a resealable plastic bag.
4. Zip the bag and shake well to coat.
5. Divide the chicken in the two crisper plates in a single layer.
6. Return the crisper plate to the Ninja Foodi Dual Zone Air Fryer.
7. Choose the Air Fry mode for Zone 1 and set the temperature to 390 degrees F and the time to 20 minutes.
8. Select the "MATCH" button to copy the settings for Zone 2.
9. Initiate cooking by pressing the START/STOP button.
10. Flip the chicken once cooked halfway through.
11. Top the chicken with reserved mayo sauce.
12. Garnish with green onions and serve warm.

Nutrition Info:

- (Per serving) Calories 374 | Fat 13g |Sodium 552mg | Carbs 25g | Fiber 1.2g | Sugar 1.2g | Protein 37.7g

Chicken Kebabs

Servings: 4
Cooking Time: 9 Minutes

Ingredients:

- 455g boneless chicken breast, cut into 1-inch pieces
- 1 tablespoon avocado oil
- 1 tablespoon Tamari soy sauce
- 1 teaspoon garlic powder
- 1 teaspoon ground ginger
- 1 teaspoon chili powder
- 1 tablespoon honey
-
- 1 green capsicum, cut into 1-inch pieces
- 1 red capsicum, cut into 1-inch pieces
- 1 yellow capsicum, cut into 1-inch pieces
- 1 courgette, cut into 1-inch pieces
- 1 small red onion, cut into 1-inch pieces
- cooking spray

Directions:

1. Rub chicken with oil and place in a bowl.
2. Mix honey, chili powder, ginger, garlic and soy sauce in a bowl.
3. Pour this mixture over the chicken.
4. Cover and marinate the chicken for 15 minutes.
5. Thread the marinated chicken with veggies on wooden skewers alternately.
6. Divide the skewers and place in the air fryer baskets.
7. Return the air fryer basket 1 to Zone 1, and basket 2 to Zone 2 of the Ninja Foodi 2-Basket Air Fryer.
8. Choose the "Air Fry" mode for Zone 1 at 350 degrees F and 9 minutes of cooking time.
9. Select the "MATCH COOK" option to copy the settings for Zone 2.
10. Initiate cooking by pressing the START/PAUSE BUTTON.
11. Flip the skewers once cooked halfway through.
12. Serve warm.

Nutrition Info:

- (Per serving) Calories 546 | Fat 33.1g |Sodium 1201mg | Carbs 30g | Fiber 2.4g | Sugar 9.7g | Protein 32g

Sweet-and-sour Chicken With Pineapple Cauliflower Rice

Servings:4
Cooking Time: 30 Minutes

Ingredients:

- FOR THE CHICKEN
- ¼ cup cornstarch, plus 2 teaspoons
- ¼ teaspoon kosher salt
- 2 large eggs
- 1 tablespoon sesame oil
- 1½ pounds boneless, skinless chicken breasts, cut into 1-inch pieces
- Nonstick cooking spray
- 6 tablespoons ketchup
- ¾ cup apple cider vinegar
- 1½ tablespoons soy sauce
- 1 tablespoon sugar
- FOR THE CAULIFLOWER RICE
- 1 cup finely diced fresh pineapple
- 1 red bell pepper, thinly sliced
- 1 small red onion, thinly sliced
- 1 tablespoon vegetable oil
- 2 cups frozen cauliflower rice, thawed
- 2 tablespoons soy sauce
- 1 teaspoon sesame oil
- 2 scallions, sliced

Directions:

1. To prep the chicken: Set up a breading station with two small shallow bowls. Combine ¼ cup of cornstarch and the salt in the first bowl. In the second bowl, beat the eggs with the sesame oil.
2. Dip the chicken pieces in the cornstarch mixture to coat, then into the egg mixture, then back into the cornstarch mixture to coat. Mist the coated pieces with cooking spray.
3. In a small bowl, whisk together the ketchup, vinegar, soy sauce, sugar, and remaining 2 teaspoons of cornstarch.
4. To prep the cauliflower rice: Blot the pineapple dry with a paper towel. In a large bowl, combine the pineapple, bell pepper, onion, and vegetable oil.
5. To cook the chicken and cauliflower rice: Install a crisper plate in each of the two baskets. Place the chicken in the Zone 1 basket and insert the basket in the unit. Place a piece of aluminum foil over the crisper plate in the Zone 2 basket and add the pineapple mixture. Insert the basket in the unit.
6. Select Zone 1, select AIR FRY, set the temperature to 400°F, and set the time to 30 minutes.
7. Select Zone 2, select AIR BROIL, set the temperature to 450°F, and set the time to 12 minutes. Select SMART FINISH.
8. Press START/PAUSE to begin cooking.
9. When the Zone 2 timer reads 4 minutes, press START/PAUSE. Remove the basket and stir in the cauliflower rice, soy sauce, and sesame oil. Reinsert the basket and press START/PAUSE to resume cooking.
10. When cooking is complete, the chicken will be golden brown and cooked through and the rice warmed through. Stir the scallions into the rice and serve.

Nutrition Info:

- (Per serving) Calories: 457; Total fat: 17g; Saturated fat: 2.5g; Carbohydrates: 31g; Fiber: 2.5g; Protein: 43g; Sodium: 1,526mg

Brazilian Chicken Drumsticks

Servings: 6
Cooking Time: 47 Minutes.

Ingredients:

- 2 teaspoons cumin seeds
- 2 teaspoons dried parsley
- 2 teaspoons turmeric powder
- 2 teaspoons dried oregano leaves
- 2 teaspoons salt
- 1 teaspoon coriander seeds
-
- 1 teaspoon black peppercorns
- 1 teaspoon cayenne pepper
- ½ cup lime juice
- 4 tablespoons vegetable oil
- 3 lbs. chicken drumsticks

Directions:

1. Grind cumin, parsley, salt, coriander seeds, cayenne pepper, peppercorns, oregano, and turmeric in a food processor.
2. Add this mixture to lemon juice and oil in a bowl and mix well.
3. Rub the spice paste over the chicken drumsticks and let them marinate for 30 minutes.
4. Divide the chicken drumsticks in both the crisper plates.
5. Return the crisper plates to the Ninja Foodi Dual Zone Air Fryer.
6. Choose the Air Fry mode for Zone 1 and set the temperature to 390 degrees F and the time to 47 minutes.
7. Select the "MATCH" button to copy the settings for Zone 2.
8. Initiate cooking by pressing the START/STOP button.
9. Flip the drumsticks when cooked halfway through, then resume cooking.
10. Serve warm.

Nutrition Info:

- (Per serving) Calories 456 | Fat 16.4g |Sodium 1321mg | Carbs 19.2g | Fiber 2.2g | Sugar 4.2g | Protein 55.2g

Buttermilk Fried Chicken

Servings: 6
Cooking Time: 30 Minutes

Ingredients:

- 1½ pounds boneless, skinless chicken thighs
- 2 cups buttermilk
- 1 cup all-purpose flour
- 1 tablespoon seasoned salt
- ½ tablespoon ground black pepper
- 1 cup panko breadcrumbs
- Cooking spray

Directions:

1. Place the chicken thighs in a shallow baking dish. Cover with the buttermilk. Refrigerate for 4 hours or overnight.
2. In a large gallon-sized resealable bag, combine the flour, seasoned salt, and pepper.
3. Remove the chicken from the buttermilk but don't discard the mixture.
4. Add the chicken to the bag and shake well to coat.
5. Dip the thighs in the buttermilk again, then coat in the panko breadcrumbs.
6. Install a crisper plate in each drawer. Place half the chicken thighs in the zone 1 drawer and half in zone 2's, then insert the drawers into the unit.
7. Select zone 1, select AIR FRY, set temperature to 390 degrees F/ 200 degrees C, and set time to 30 minutes. Select MATCH to match zone 2 settings to zone 1. Press the START/STOP button to begin cooking.
8. When the time reaches 15 minutes, press START/STOP to pause the unit. Remove the drawers and flip the chicken. Re-insert the drawers into the unit and press START/STOP to resume cooking.
9. When cooking is complete, remove the chicken.

Nutrition Info:

- (Per serving) Calories 335 | Fat 12.8g | Sodium 687mg | Carbs 33.1g | Fiber 0.4g | Sugar 4g | Protein 24.5g

Air-fried Turkey Breast With Roasted Green Bean Casserole

Servings:4

Cooking Time: 50 Minutes

Ingredients:

- FOR THE TURKEY BREAST
- 2 teaspoons unsalted butter, at room temperature
- 1 bone-in split turkey breast (3 pounds), thawed if frozen
- 1 teaspoon poultry seasoning
- ½ teaspoon kosher salt
- ⅓ teaspoon freshly ground black pepper
- FOR THE GREEN BEAN CASSEROLE
- 1 (10.5-ounce) can condensed cream of mushroom soup
- ½ cup whole milk
- 1 cup store-bought crispy fried onions, divided
- ¼ teaspoon kosher salt
- ¼ teaspoon freshly ground black pepper
- 1 pound green beans, trimmed
- ¼ cup panko bread crumbs
- Nonstick cooking spray

Directions:

1. To prep the turkey breast: Spread the butter over the skin side of the turkey. Season with the poultry seasoning, salt, and black pepper.
2. To prep the green bean casserole: In a medium bowl, combine the soup, milk, ½ cup of crispy onions, the salt, and black pepper.
3. To cook the turkey and beans: Install a crisper plate in the Zone 1 basket. Place the turkey skin-side up in the basket and insert the basket in the unit. Place the green beans in the Zone 2 basket and insert the basket in the unit.
4. Select Zone 1, select AIR FRY, set the temperature to 360°F, and set the time to 50 minutes.
5. Select Zone 2, select ROAST, set the temperature to 350°F, and set the time to 40 minutes. Select SMART FINISH.
6. Press START/PAUSE to begin cooking.
7. When the Zone 2 timer reads 30 minutes, press START/PAUSE. Remove the basket and stir the soup mixture into the beans. Scatter the panko and remaining ½ cup of crispy onions over the top, then spritz with cooking spray. Reinsert the basket and press START/PAUSE to resume cooking.
8. When cooking is complete, the turkey will be cooked through (an instant-read thermometer should read 165°F) and the green bean casserole will be bubbling and golden brown on top.
9. Let the turkey and casserole rest for at least 15 minutes before serving.

Nutrition Info:

- (Per serving) Calories: 577; Total fat: 22g; Saturated fat: 6.5g; Carbohydrates: 24g; Fiber: 3.5g; Protein: 68g; Sodium: 1,165mg

Cornish Hen With Asparagus

Servings:2
Cooking Time:45

Ingredients:

- 10 spears of asparagus
- Salt and black pepper, to taste
- 1 Cornish hen
- Salt, to taste
- Black pepper, to taste
- 1 teaspoon of Paprika
- Coconut spray, for greasing
- 2 lemons, sliced

Directions:

1. Wash and pat dry the asparagus and coat it with coconut oil spray.
2. Sprinkle salt on the asparagus and place inside the first basket of the air fryer.
3. Next, take the Cornish hen and rub it well with the salt, black pepper, and paprika.
4. Oil sprays the Cornish hen and place in the second air fryer basket.
5. Press button 1 for the first basket and set it to AIR FRY mode at 350 degrees F, for 8 minutes.
6. For the second basket hit 2 and set the time to 45 minutes at 350 degrees F, by selecting the ROAST mode.
7. To start cooking, hit the smart finish button and press hit start.
8. Once the 6 minutes pass press 1 and pause and take out the asparagus.
9. Once the chicken cooking cycle complete, press 2 and hit pause.
10. Take out the Basket of chicken and let it transfer to the serving plate
11. Serve the chicken with roasted asparagus and slices of lemon.
12. Serve hot and enjoy.

Nutrition Info:

- (Per serving) Calories 192| Fat 4.7g| Sodium 151mg | Carbs10.7 g | Fiber 4.6g | Sugar 3.8g | Protein 30g

Wings With Corn On The Cob

Servings: 2
Cooking Time: 40 Minutes

Ingredients:

- 6 chicken wings, skinless
- 2 tablespoons coconut amino
- 2 tablespoons brown sugar
- 1 teaspoon ginger, paste
- ½ inch garlic, minced
- Salt and black pepper to taste
- 2 corn on cobs, small
- Oil spray, for greasing

Directions:

1. Spray the corns with oil spray and season them with salt.
2. Coat the chicken wings with coconut amino, brown sugar, ginger, garlic, salt, and black pepper.
3. Spray the wings with a good amount of oil spray.
4. Put the chicken wings in the zone 1 basket.
5. Put the corn into the zone 2 basket.
6. Select ROAST mode for the chicken wings and set the time to 23 minutes at 400 degrees F/ 200 degrees C.
7. Press 2 and select the AIR FRY mode for the corn and set the time to 40 at 300 degrees F/ 150 degrees C.
8. Once it's done, serve and enjoy.

Nutrition Info:

- (Per serving) Calories 950 | Fat 33.4g | Sodium 592 mg | Carbs 27.4g | Fiber 2.1g | Sugar 11.3 g | Protein 129g

Balsamic Duck Breast

Servings: 2
Cooking Time: 20 Minutes.

Ingredients:

- 2 duck breasts
- 1 teaspoon parsley
- Salt and black pepper, to taste
- Marinade:
- 1 tablespoon olive oil
- ½ teaspoon French mustard
- 1 teaspoon dried garlic
- 2 teaspoons honey
- ½ teaspoon balsamic vinegar

Directions:

1. Mix olive oil, mustard, garlic, honey, and balsamic vinegar in a bowl.
2. Add duck breasts to the marinade and rub well.
3. Place one duck breast in each crisper plate.
4. Return the crisper plates to the Ninja Foodi Dual Zone Air Fryer.
5. Choose the Air Fry mode for Zone 1 and set the temperature to 360 degrees F and the time to 20 minutes.
6. Select the "MATCH" button to copy the settings for Zone 2.
7. Initiate cooking by pressing the START/STOP button.
8. Flip the duck breasts once cooked halfway through, then resume cooking.
9. Serve warm.

Nutrition Info:

- (Per serving) Calories 546 | Fat 33.1g |Sodium 1201mg | Carbs 30g | Fiber 2.4g | Sugar 9.7g | Protein 32g

Juicy Duck Breast

Servings: 1
Cooking Time: 20 Minutes

Ingredients:

- ½ duck breast
- Salt and black pepper, to taste
- 2 tablespoons plum sauce

Directions:

1. Rub the duck breast with black pepper and salt.
2. Place the duck breast in air fryer basket 1 and add plum sauce on top.
3. Return the basket to the Ninja Foodi 2 Baskets Air Fryer.
4. Choose the "Air Fry" mode for Zone 1 and set the temperature to 400 degrees F and 20 minutes of cooking time.
5. Initiate cooking by pressing the START/PAUSE BUTTON.
6. Flip the duck breast once cooked halfway through.
7. Serve warm.

Nutrition Info:

- (Per serving) Calories 379 | Fat 19g |Sodium 184mg | Carbs 12.3g | Fiber 0.6g | Sugar 2g | Protein 37.7g

Chili Chicken Wings

Servings: 4
Cooking Time: 43 Minutes.

Ingredients:

- 8 chicken wings drumettes
- cooking spray
- ⅛ cup low-fat buttermilk
- ¼ cup almond flour
- McCormick Chicken Seasoning to taste
- Thai Chili Marinade
- 1 ½ tablespoons low-sodium soy sauce
-
- ½ teaspoon ginger, minced
- 1 ½ garlic cloves
- 1 green onion
- ½ teaspoon rice wine vinegar
- ½ tablespoon Sriracha sauce
- ½ tablespoon sesame oil

Directions:

1. Put all the ingredients for the marinade in the blender and blend them for 1 minute.
2. Keep this marinade aside. Pat dry the washed chicken and place it in the Ziploc bag.
3. Add buttermilk, chicken seasoning, and zip the bag.
4. Shake the bag well, then refrigerator for 30 minutes for marination.
5. Remove the chicken drumettes from the marinade, then dredge them through dry flour.
6. Spread the drumettes in the two crisper plate and spray them with cooking oil.
7. Return the crisper plate to the Ninja Foodi Dual Zone Air Fryer.
8. Choose the Air Fry mode for Zone 1 and set the temperature to 390 degrees F and the time to 43 minutes.
9. Select the "MATCH" button to copy the settings for Zone 2.
10. Initiate cooking by pressing the START/STOP button.
11. Toss the drumettes once cooked halfway through.
12. Now brush the chicken pieces with Thai chili sauce and then resume cooking.
13. Serve warm.

Nutrition Info:

- (Per serving) Calories 223 | Fat 11.7g |Sodium 721mg | Carbs 13.6g | Fiber 0.7g | Sugar 8g | Protein 15.7g

Chicken Parmesan

Servings: 4
Cooking Time: 20 Minutes

Ingredients:

- 2 large eggs
- ½ cup seasoned breadcrumbs
- 1/3 cup grated parmesan cheese
- ¼ teaspoon pepper
- 4 boneless, skinless chicken breast halves (6 ounces each)
- 1 cup pasta sauce
- 1 cup shredded mozzarella cheese
- Chopped fresh basil (optional)
-

Directions:

1. Lightly beat the eggs in a small bowl.
2. Combine the breadcrumbs, parmesan cheese, and pepper in a shallow bowl.
3. After dipping the chicken in the egg, coat it in the crumb mixture.
4. Install a crisper plate in both drawers. Place half the chicken breasts in the zone 1 drawer and half in zone 2's, then insert the drawers into the unit.
5. Select zone 1, select AIR FRY, set temperature to 390 degrees F/ 200 degrees C, and set time to 20 minutes. Select MATCH to match zone 2 settings to zone 1. Press the START/STOP button to begin cooking.
6. When the time reaches 10 minutes, press START/STOP to pause the unit. Remove the drawers and flip the chicken. Re-insert the drawers into the unit and press START/STOP to resume cooking.
7. When cooking is complete, remove the chicken.

Nutrition Info:

- (Per serving) Calories 293 | Fat 15.8g | Sodium 203mg | Carbs 11.1g | Fiber 2.4g | Sugar 8.7g | Protein 29g

Chicken Fajitas With Street Corn

Servings:4

Cooking Time: 20 Minutes

Ingredients:

- FOR THE FAJITAS
- 1½ pounds boneless, skinless chicken breasts, cut into strips
- 2 bell peppers (red, orange, yellow, or a combination), sliced into ½-inch-wide strips
- 1 small red onion, sliced
- 1 tablespoon vegetable oil
- 2 teaspoons chili powder
- 1 teaspoon ground cumin
- 1 teaspoon kosher salt
- ½ teaspoon freshly ground black pepper
- ½ teaspoon paprika
- ¼ cup fresh cilantro, chopped
- Juice of 1 lime
- 8 (6-inch) flour tortillas
- FOR THE CORN
- ¼ cup mayonnaise
- ¼ cup sour cream
- ¼ cup crumbled Cotija or feta cheese
- 2 tablespoons chopped fresh cilantro
- 1 teaspoon minced garlic
- ½ teaspoon chili powder
- 4 ears corn, husked

Directions:

1. To prep the fajitas: In a large bowl, combine the chicken, bell peppers, onion, oil, chili powder, cumin, salt, black pepper, and paprika and toss to coat.
2. To prep the corn: In a shallow dish, combine the mayonnaise, sour cream, cheese, cilantro, garlic, and chili powder. Mix well and set aside.
3. To cook the fajitas and corn: Install a crisper plate in each of the two baskets. Place the fajita filling in the Zone 1 basket and insert the basket in the unit. Place the corn ears in the Zone 2 basket and insert the basket in the unit.
4. Select Zone 1, select AIR FRY, set the temperature to 390°F, and set the time to 20 minutes.
5. Select Zone 2, select AIR BROIL, set the temperature to 450°F, and set the time to 12 minutes. Select SMART FINISH.
6. Press START/PAUSE to begin cooking.
7. When both timers read 6 minutes, press START/PAUSE. Remove the Zone 1 basket, shake to redistribute the fajita filling, and reinsert the basket. Remove the Zone 2 basket and use silicone-tipped tongs to flip the corn. Reinsert the basket and press START/PAUSE to resume cooking.
8. When cooking is complete, the chicken will be fully cooked and the vegetables will be slightly charred.
9. Mix the cilantro and lime juice into the fajita filling. Divide the filling among the tortillas. Roll the corn in the mayonnaise and cheese mixture to coat. Serve hot.

Nutrition Info:

- (Per serving) Calories: 705; Total fat: 29g; Saturated fat: 8g; Carbohydrates: 60g; Fiber: 5g; Protein: 51g; Sodium: 1,155mg

Chapter 6 Fish And Seafood Recipes

Tilapia With Mojo And Crispy Plantains

Servings:4
Cooking Time: 30 Minutes
Ingredients:

- FOR THE TILAPIA
- 4 tilapia fillets (6 ounces each)
- 2 tablespoons all-purpose flour
- Nonstick cooking spray
- ¼ cup freshly squeezed orange juice
- 3 tablespoons fresh lime juice
- 2 tablespoons olive oil
- 1 tablespoon minced garlic
- ½ teaspoon ground cumin
- ¼ teaspoon kosher salt
- FOR THE PLANTAINS
- 1 large green plantain
- 2 cups cold water
- 2 teaspoons kosher salt
- Nonstick cooking spray

Directions:

1. To prep the tilapia: Dust both sides of the tilapia fillets with the flour, then spritz with cooking spray.
2. In a small bowl, whisk together the orange juice, lime juice, oil, garlic, cumin, and salt. Set the mojo sauce aside.
3. To prep the plantains: Cut the ends from the plantain, then remove and discard the peel. Slice the plantain into 1-inch rounds.
4. In a large bowl, combine the water, salt, and plantains. Let soak for 15 minutes.
5. Drain the plantains and pat them dry with paper towels. Spray with cooking spray.
6. To cook the tilapia and plantains: Install a crisper plate in each of the two baskets. Place the tilapia in a single layer in the Zone 1 basket (work in batches if needed) and insert the basket in the unit. Place the plantains in the Zone 2 basket and insert the basket in the unit.
7. Select Zone 1, select AIR FRY, set the temperature to 390°F, and set the timer to 10 minutes.
8. Select Zone 2, select AIR FRY, set the temperature to 390°F, and set the timer to 30 minutes. Select SMART FINISH.
9. Press START/PAUSE to begin cooking.
10. When the Zone 2 timer reads 10 minutes, press START/PAUSE. Remove the basket and use silicone-tipped tongs to transfer the plantains, which should be tender, to a cutting board. Use the bottom of a heavy glass to smash each plantain flat. Spray both sides with cooking spray and place them back in the basket. Reinsert the basket and press START/PAUSE to resume cooking.
11. When the Zone 1 timer reads 5 minutes, press START/PAUSE. Remove the basket. Spoon half of the mojo sauce over the tilapia. Reinsert the basket and press START/PAUSE to resume cooking.
12. When cooking is complete, the fish should be cooked through and the plantains crispy. Serve the tilapia and plantains with the remaining mojo sauce for dipping.

Nutrition Info:

- (Per serving) Calories: 380; Total fat: 21g; Saturated fat: 2g; Carbohydrates: 20g; Fiber: 1g; Protein: 35g; Sodium: 217mg

Herb Lemon Mussels

Servings: 6
Cooking Time: 10 Minutes
Ingredients:

- 1kg mussels, steamed & half shell
- 1 tbsp thyme, chopped
- 1 tbsp parsley, chopped
- 1 tsp dried parsley
- 1 tsp garlic, minced
-
- 60ml olive oil
- 45ml lemon juice
- Pepper
- Salt

Directions:

1. In a bowl, mix mussels with the remaining ingredients.
2. Insert a crisper plate in the Ninja Foodi air fryer baskets.
3. Add the mussels to both baskets.
4. Select zone 1 then select "air fry" mode and set the temperature to 360 degrees F for 10 minutes. Press "match" to match zone 2 settings to zone 1. Press "start/stop" to begin.

Nutrition Info:

- (Per serving) Calories 206 | Fat 11.9g |Sodium 462mg | Carbs 6.3g | Fiber 0.3g | Sugar 0.2g | Protein 18.2g

Blackened Mahimahi With Honey-roasted Carrots

Servings:4
Cooking Time: 30 Minutes
Ingredients:

- FOR THE MAHIMAHI
- 4 mahimahi fillets (4 ounces each)
- 1 tablespoon olive oil
- 1 tablespoon blackening seasoning
- Lemon wedges, for serving
- FOR THE CARROTS
- 1 pound carrots, peeled and cut into ½-inch rounds
- 2 teaspoons vegetable oil
- ½ teaspoon kosher salt
- ¼ teaspoon freshly ground black pepper
- 1 tablespoon salted butter, cut into small pieces
- 1 tablespoon honey
- 2 tablespoons chopped fresh parsley

Directions:

1. To prep the mahimahi: Brush both sides of the fish with the oil and sprinkle with the blackening seasoning.
2. To prep the carrots: In a large bowl, combine the carrots, oil, salt, and black pepper. Stir well to coat the carrots with the oil.
3. To cook the mahimahi and carrots: Install a crisper plate in each of the two baskets. Place the fish in the Zone 1 basket and insert the basket in the unit. Place the carrots in the Zone 2 basket and insert the basket in the unit.
4. Select Zone 1, select AIR FRY, set the temperature to 380°F, and set the timer to 14 minutes.
5. Select Zone 2, select ROAST, set the temperature to 400°F, and set the timer to 30 minutes. Select SMART FINISH.
6. Press START/PAUSE to begin cooking.
7. When the Zone 2 timer reads 15 minutes, press START/PAUSE. Remove the basket and scatter the butter over the carrots, then drizzle them with the honey. Reinsert the basket and press START/PAUSE to resume cooking.
8. When cooking is complete, the fish should be cooked through and the carrots soft.
9. Stir the parsley into the carrots. Serve the fish with lemon wedges.

Nutrition Info:

- (Per serving) Calories: 235; Total fat: 9.5g; Saturated fat: 3g; Carbohydrates: 15g; Fiber: 3g; Protein: 22g; Sodium: 672mg

Shrimp Po'boys With Sweet Potato Fries

Servings:4
Cooking Time: 30 Minutes
Ingredients:

- FOR THE SHRIMP PO'BOYS
- ½ cup buttermilk
- 1 tablespoon Louisiana-style hot sauce
- ¾ cup all-purpose flour
- ½ cup cornmeal
- ½ teaspoon kosher salt
- ½ teaspoon paprika
- ½ teaspoon garlic powder
- ½ teaspoon freshly ground black pepper
- 1 pound peeled medium shrimp, thawed if frozen
- Nonstock cooking spray
- ½ cup store-bought rémoulade sauce
- 4 French bread rolls, halved lengthwise
- ½ cup shredded lettuce
- 1 tomato, sliced
- FOR THE SWEET POTATO FRIES
- 2 medium sweet potatoes
- 2 teaspoons vegetable oil
- ¼ teaspoon garlic powder
- ¼ teaspoon paprika
- ¼ teaspoon kosher salt

Directions:

1. To prep the shrimp: In a medium bowl, combine the buttermilk and hot sauce. In a shallow bowl, combine the flour, cornmeal, salt, paprika, garlic powder, and black pepper.
2. Add the shrimp to the buttermilk and stir to coat. Remove the shrimp, letting the excess buttermilk drip off, then add to the cornmeal mixture to coat.
3. Spritz the breaded shrimp with cooking spray, then let sit for 10 minutes.
4. To prep the sweet potatoes: Peel the sweet potatoes and cut them lengthwise into ¼-inch-thick sticks (like shoestring fries).
5. In a large bowl, combine the sweet potatoes, oil, garlic powder, paprika, and salt. Toss to coat.
6. To cook the shrimp and fries: Install a crisper plate in each of the two baskets. Place the shrimp in the Zone 1 basket and insert the basket in the unit. Place the sweet potatoes in a single layer in the Zone 2 basket and insert the basket in the unit.
7. Select Zone 1, select AIR FRY, set the temperature to 390°F, and set the timer to 13 minutes.
8. Select Zone 2, select AIR FRY, set the temperature to 400°F, and set the timer to 30 minutes. Select SMART FINISH.
9. Press START/PAUSE to begin cooking.
10. When cooking is complete, the shrimp should be golden and cooked through and the sweet potato fries crisp.
11. Spread the rémoulade on the cut sides of the rolls. Divide the lettuce and tomato among the rolls, then top with the fried shrimp. Serve with the sweet potato fries on the side.

Nutrition Info:

- (Per serving) Calories: 669; Total fat: 22g; Saturated fat: 2g; Carbohydrates: 86g; Fiber: 3.5g; Protein: 33g; Sodium: 1,020mg

Salmon Nuggets

Servings: 4
Cooking Time: 15 Minutes.

Ingredients:

- ⅓ cup maple syrup
- ¼ teaspoon dried chipotle pepper
- 1 pinch sea salt
- 1 ½ cups croutons
-
- 1 large egg
- 1 (1 pound) skinless salmon fillet, cut into 1 ½-inch chunk
- cooking spray

Directions:

1. Mix chipotle powder, maple syrup, and salt in a saucepan and cook on a simmer for 5 minutes.
2. Crush the croutons in a food processor and transfer to a bowl.
3. Beat egg in another shallow bowl.
4. Season the salmon chunks with sea salt.
5. Dip the salmon in the egg, then coat with breadcrumbs.
6. Divide the coated salmon chunks in the two crisper plates.
7. Return the crisper plate to the Ninja Foodi Dual Zone Air Fryer.
8. Select the Air Fry mode for Zone 1 and set the temperature to 390 degrees F and the time to 10 minutes.
9. Press the "MATCH" button to copy the settings for Zone 2.
10. Initiate cooking by pressing the START/STOP button.
11. Flip the chunks once cooked halfway through, then resume cooking.
12. Pour the maple syrup on top and serve warm.

Nutrition Info:

- (Per serving) Calories 275 | Fat 1.4g |Sodium 582mg | Carbs 31.5g | Fiber 1.1g | Sugar 0.1g | Protein 29.8g

Pretzel-crusted Catfish

Servings: 4
Cooking Time: 12 Minutes

Ingredients:

- 4 catfish fillets
- ½ teaspoon salt
- ½ teaspoon black pepper
- 2 large eggs
- ⅓ cup Dijon mustard
- 2 tablespoons 2% milk
- ½ cup all-purpose flour
- 4 cups miniature pretzels, crushed
- Cooking spray
- Lemon slices

Directions:

1. Rub the catfish with black pepper and salt.
2. Beat eggs with milk and mustard in a bowl.
3. Spread pretzels and flour in two separate bowls.
4. Coat the catfish with flour then dip in the egg mixture and coat with the pretzels.
5. Place two fish fillets in each air fryer basket.
6. Return the air fryer basket 1 to Zone 1, and basket 2 to Zone 2 of the Ninja Foodi 2-Basket Air Fryer.
7. Choose the "Air Fry" mode for Zone 1 at 325 degrees F and 12 minutes of cooking time.
8. Select the "MATCH COOK" option to copy the settings for Zone 2.
9. Initiate cooking by pressing the START/PAUSE BUTTON.
10. Serve warm.

Nutrition Info:

- (Per serving) Calories 196 | Fat 7.1g |Sodium 492mg | Carbs 21.6g | Fiber 2.9g | Sugar 0.8g | Protein 13.4g

Garlic Shrimp With Pasta Alfredo

Servings:4
Cooking Time: 40 Minutes
Ingredients:

- FOR THE GARLIC SHRIMP
- 1 pound peeled small shrimp, thawed if frozen
- 1 tablespoon olive oil
- 1 tablespoon minced garlic
- ¼ teaspoon sea salt
- ¼ cup chopped fresh parsley
- FOR THE PASTA ALFREDO
- 8 ounces no-boil lasagna noodles
- 2 cups whole milk
- ¼ cup heavy (whipping) cream
- 2 tablespoons unsalted butter, cut into small pieces
- 1 tablespoon minced garlic
- ½ teaspoon kosher salt
- ¼ teaspoon freshly ground black pepper
- ½ cup grated Parmesan cheese

Directions:

1. To prep the garlic shrimp: In a large bowl, combine the shrimp, oil, garlic, and salt.
2. To prep the pasta alfredo: Break the lasagna noodles into 2-inch pieces. Add the milk to the Zone 2 basket, then add the noodles, cream, butter, garlic, salt, and black pepper. Stir well and ensure the pasta is fully submerged in the liquid.
3. To cook the shrimp and pasta: Install a crisper plate in the Zone 1 basket. Place the shrimp in the basket and insert the basket in the unit. Insert the Zone 2 basket in the unit.
4. Select Zone 1, select AIR FRY, set the temperature to 390°F, and set the timer to 13 minutes.
5. Select Zone 2, select BAKE, set the temperature to 360°F, and set the timer to 40 minutes. Select SMART FINISH.
6. Press START/PAUSE to begin cooking.
7. When the Zone 2 timer reads 20 minutes, press START/PAUSE. Remove the basket and stir the pasta. Reinsert the basket and press START/PAUSE to resume cooking.
8. When cooking is complete, the shrimp will be cooked through and the pasta tender.
9. Transfer the pasta to a serving dish and stir in the Parmesan. Top with the shrimp and parsley.

Nutrition Info:

- (Per serving) Calories: 542; Total fat: 23g; Saturated fat: 11g; Carbohydrates: 52g; Fiber: 2g; Protein: 34g; Sodium: 643mg

Herb Tuna Patties

Servings: 10
Cooking Time: 12 Minutes
Ingredients:

- 2 eggs
- 425g can tuna, drained & diced
- ½ tsp garlic powder
- ½ small onion, minced
- 1 celery stalk, chopped
- 42g parmesan cheese, grated
- 50g breadcrumbs
- ½ tsp dried oregano
- ½ tsp dried basil
- ½ tsp dried thyme
- 15ml lemon juice
- 1 lemon zest
- Pepper
- Salt

Directions:

1. In a bowl, mix tuna with remaining ingredients until well combined.
2. Insert a crisper plate in the Ninja Foodi air fryer baskets.
3. Make patties from the tuna mixture and place them in both baskets.
4. Select zone 1, then select "bake" mode and set the temperature to 380 degrees F for 12 minutes. Press "match" to match zone 2 settings to zone 1. Press "start/stop" to begin. Turn halfway through.

Nutrition Info:

- (Per serving) Calories 86 | Fat 1.5g |Sodium 90mg | Carbs 4.5g | Fiber 0.4g | Sugar 0.6g | Protein 12.8g

Shrimp With Lemon And Pepper

Servings: 4
Cooking Time: 8 Minutes

Ingredients:

- 455g raw shrimp, peeled and deveined
- 118ml olive oil
- 2 tablespoons lemon juice
- 1 teaspoon black pepper
- ½ teaspoon salt

Directions:

1. Toss shrimp with black pepper, salt, lemon juice and oil in a bowl.
2. Divide the shrimp into the Ninja Foodi 2 Baskets Air Fryer baskets.
3. Return the air fryer basket 1 to Zone 1, and basket 2 to Zone 2 of the Ninja Foodi 2-Basket Air Fryer.
4. Choose the "Air Fry" mode for Zone 1 at 350 degrees F and 8 minutes of cooking time.
5. Select the "MATCH COOK" option to copy the settings for Zone 2.
6. Initiate cooking by pressing the START/PAUSE BUTTON.
7. Serve warm.

Nutrition Info:

- (Per serving) Calories 257 | Fat 10.4g |Sodium 431mg | Carbs 20g | Fiber 0g | Sugar 1.6g | Protein 21g

Salmon With Green Beans

Servings:1
Cooking Time:18

Ingredients:

- 1 salmon fillet, 2 inches thick
- 2 teaspoons of olive oil
- 2 teaspoons of smoked paprika
- Salt and black pepper, to taste
- 1 cup green beans
- Oil spray, for greasing

Directions:

1. Grease the green beans with oil spray and add them to zone 1 basket.
2. Now rub the salmon fillet with olive oil, smoked paprika, salt, and black pepper.
3. Put the salmon fillets in the zone 2 basket.
4. Now set the zone one basket to AIRFRY mode at 350 degrees F for 18 minutes.
5. Set the Zone 2 basket to 390 degrees F for 16-18 minutes
6. Hit the smart finish button.
7. Once done, take out the salmon and green beans and transfer them to the serving plates and enjoy.

Nutrition Info:

- (Per serving) Calories 367| Fat22 g| Sodium 87mg | Carbs 10.2g | Fiber 5.3g | Sugar 2g | Protein 37.2g

Furikake Salmon

Servings: 4
Cooking Time: 10 Minutes

Ingredients:

- ½ cup mayonnaise
- 1 tablespoon shoyu
- 455gsalmon fillet
- Salt and black pepper to taste
- 2 tablespoons furikake

Directions:

1. Mix shoyu with mayonnaise in a small bowl.
2. Rub the salmon with black pepper and salt.
3. Place the salmon pieces in the air fryer baskets.
4. Top them with the mayo mixture.
5. Return the air fryer basket 1 to Zone 1, and basket 2 to Zone 2 of the Ninja Foodi 2-Basket Air Fryer.
6. Choose the "Air Fry" mode for Zone 1 at 400 degrees F and 10 minutes of cooking time.
7. Select the "MATCH COOK" option to copy the settings for Zone 2.
8. Initiate cooking by pressing the START/PAUSE BUTTON.
9. Serve warm.

Nutrition Info:

- (Per serving) Calories 297 | Fat 1g |Sodium 291mg | Carbs 35g | Fiber 1g | Sugar 9g | Protein 29g

Roasted Salmon And Parmesan Asparagus

Servings: 4
Cooking Time: 27 Minutes

Ingredients:

- 2 tablespoons Montreal steak seasoning
- 3 tablespoons brown sugar
- 3 uncooked salmon fillets (6 ounces each)
- 2 tablespoons canola oil, divided
- 1-pound asparagus, ends trimmed
- Kosher salt, as desired
- Ground black pepper, as desired
- ¼ cup shredded parmesan cheese, divided

Directions:

1. Combine the steak spice and brown sugar in a small bowl.
2. Brush 1 tablespoon of oil over the salmon fillets, then thoroughly coat with the sugar mixture.
3. Toss the asparagus with the remaining 1 tablespoon of oil, salt, and pepper in a mixing bowl.
4. Place a crisper plate in both drawers. Put the fillets skin-side down in the zone 1 drawer, then place the drawer in the unit. Insert the zone 2 drawer into the device after placing the asparagus in it.
5. Select zone 1, then ROAST, then set the temperature to 390 degrees F/ 200 degrees C with a 17-minute timer. To match the zone 2 settings to zone 1, choose MATCH. To begin cooking, press the START/STOP button.
6. When the zone 2 timer reaches 7 minutes, press START/STOP. Remove the zone 2 drawer from the unit. Flip the asparagus with silicone-tipped tongs. Re-insert the drawer into the unit. Continue cooking by pressing START/STOP.
7. When the zone 2 timer has reached 14 minutes, press START/STOP. Remove the zone 2 drawer from the unit. Sprinkle half the parmesan cheese over the asparagus, and mix lightly. Re-insert the drawer into the unit. Continue cooking by pressing START/STOP.
8. Transfer the fillets and asparagus to a serving plate once they've finished cooking. Serve with the remaining parmesan cheese on top of the asparagus.

Nutrition Info:

- (Per serving) Calories 293 | Fat 15.8g | Sodium 203mg | Carbs 11.1g | Fiber 2.4g | Sugar 8.7g | Protein 29g

Glazed Scallops

Servings: 6
Cooking Time: 13 Minutes.

Ingredients:

- 12 scallops
- 3 tablespoons olive oil
- Black pepper and salt to taste

Directions:

1. Rub the scallops with olive oil, black pepper, and salt.
2. Divide the scallops in the two crisper plates.
3. Return the crisper plate to the Ninja Foodi Dual Zone Air Fryer.
4. Choose the Air Fry mode for Zone 1 and set the temperature to 390 degrees F and the time to 13 minutes.
5. Select the "MATCH" button to copy the settings for Zone 2.
6. Initiate cooking by pressing the START/STOP button.
7. Flip the scallops once cooked halfway through, and resume cooking.
8. Serve warm.

Nutrition Info:

- (Per serving) Calories 308 | Fat 24g |Sodium 715mg | Carbs 0.8g | Fiber 0.1g | Sugar 0.1g | Protein 21.9g

Lemon Pepper Fish Fillets

Servings: 4
Cooking Time: 10 Minutes

Ingredients:

- 4 tilapia fillets
- 30ml olive oil
- 2 tbsp lemon zest
- ⅛ tsp paprika
- 1 tsp garlic, minced
- 1 ½ tsp ground peppercorns
- Pepper
- Salt

Directions:

1. In a small bowl, mix oil, peppercorns, paprika, garlic, lemon zest, pepper, and salt.
2. Brush the fish fillets with oil mixture.
3. Insert a crisper plate in the Ninja Foodi air fryer baskets.
4. Place fish fillets in both baskets.
5. Select zone 1 then select "air fry" mode and set the temperature to 390 degrees F for 10 minutes. Press "match" to match zone 2 settings to zone 1. Press "start/stop" to begin.

Nutrition Info:

- (Per serving) Calories 203 | Fat 9g |Sodium 99mg | Carbs 0.9g | Fiber 0.2g | Sugar 0.2g | Protein 32.1g

Tuna Patties

Servings: 6
Cooking Time: 10 Minutes

Ingredients:

- For the tuna patties:
- 1 tablespoon extra-virgin olive oil
- 1 tablespoon butter
- ½ cup chopped onion
- ½ red bell pepper, chopped
- 1 teaspoon minced garlic
- 2 (7-ounce) cans or 3 (5-ounce) cans albacore tuna fish in water, drained
- 1 tablespoon lime juice
- 1 celery stalk, chopped
- ¼ cup chopped fresh parsley
-
- 3 tablespoons grated parmesan cheese
- ½ teaspoon dried oregano
- ¼ teaspoon salt
- Black pepper, to taste
- 1 teaspoon sriracha
- ½ cup panko crumbs
- 2 whisked eggs
- For the crumb coating:
- ½ cup panko crumbs
- ¼ cup parmesan cheese
- Non-stick spray

Directions:

1. In a skillet, heat the oil and butter over medium-high heat.
2. Sauté the onions, red bell pepper, and garlic for 5 to 7 minutes.
3. Drain the tuna from the cans thoroughly. Put the tuna in a large mixing bowl. Add the lime juice.
4. Add the sautéed vegetables to the mixing bowl.
5. Add the celery, parsley, and cheese. Combine well.
6. Add the oregano, salt, and pepper to taste. Mix well.
7. Add a dash of sriracha for a spicy kick and mix well.
8. Add the panko crumbs and mix well.
9. Mix in the eggs until the mixture is well combined. You can add an extra egg if necessary, but the tuna is usually wet enough that it isn't required. Form 6 patties from the mixture.
10. Refrigerate for 30 to 60 minutes (or even overnight).
11. Remove from refrigerator and coat with a mixture of the ½ cup of panko crumbs and ¼ cup of parmesan cheese.
12. Spray the tops of the coated patties with some non-stick cooking spray.
13. Place a crisper place in each drawer. Put 3 patties in each drawer. Insert the drawers into the unit.
14. Select zone 1, then AIR FRY, then set the temperature to 390 degrees F/ 200 degrees C with a 10-minute timer. To match zone 2 settings to zone 1, choose MATCH. To begin, select START/STOP.
15. Remove and garnish with chopped parsley.

Nutrition Info:

- (Per serving) Calories 381 | Fat 16g | Sodium 1007mg | Carbs 23g | Fiber 2g | Sugar 4g | Protein 38g

Southwestern Fish Fillets

Servings: 4
Cooking Time: 16 Minutes

Ingredients:

- 455g trout fillets
- 1 tsp garlic powder
- 29g breadcrumbs
- 15ml olive oil
- 1 tsp chilli powder
- 1 tsp onion powder

Directions:

1. In a small bowl, mix breadcrumbs, garlic powder, onion powder, and chilli powder.
2. Brush fish fillets with oil and coat with breadcrumbs.
3. Insert a crisper plate in the Ninja Foodi air fryer baskets.
4. Place coated fish fillets in both baskets.
5. Select zone 1 then select "air fry" mode and set the temperature to 375 degrees F for 16 minutes. Press "match" and "start/stop" to begin.

Nutrition Info:

- (Per serving) Calories 272 | Fat 13.5g |Sodium 120mg | Carbs 5g | Fiber 0.6g | Sugar 0.7g | Protein 31.1g

Healthy Lobster Cakes

Servings: 6
Cooking Time: 12 Minutes

Ingredients:

- 1 egg
- 145g cooked lobster meat
- 60g butter, melted
- 1 tbsp Cajun seasoning
- 50g breadcrumbs
- Pepper
- Salt

Directions:

1. In a shallow dish, add breadcrumbs, pepper, and salt.
2. In a bowl, mix lobster meat, Cajun seasoning, egg, and butter until well combined.
3. Make patties from the lobster meat mixture and coat with breadcrumbs.
4. Insert a crisper plate in the Ninja Foodi air fryer baskets.
5. Place the coated patties in both baskets.
6. Select zone 1, then select "bake" mode and set the temperature to 390 degrees F for 12 minutes. Press "match" to match zone 2 settings to zone 1. Press "start/stop" to begin.

Nutrition Info:

- (Per serving) Calories 119 | Fat 7.2g |Sodium 287mg | Carbs 6.6g | Fiber 0.4g | Sugar 0.6g | Protein 6.8g

Bang Bang Shrimp

Servings: 4
Cooking Time: 20 Minutes

Ingredients:

- For the shrimp:
- 1 cup corn starch
- Salt and pepper, to taste
- 2 pounds shrimp, peeled and deveined
- ½ to 1 cup buttermilk
- Cooking oil spray
- 1 large egg whisked with 1 teaspoon water
- For the sauce:
- 1/3 cup sweet Thai chili sauce
- ¼ cup sour cream
- ¼ cup mayonnaise
- 2 tablespoons buttermilk
- 1 tablespoon sriracha, or to taste
- Pinch dried dill weed

Directions:

1. Season the corn starch with salt and pepper in a wide, shallow bowl.
2. In a large mixing bowl, toss the shrimp in the buttermilk to coat them.
3. Dredge the shrimp in the seasoned corn starch.
4. Brush with the egg wash after spraying with cooking oil.
5. Place a crisper plate in each drawer. Place the shrimp in a single layer in each. You may need to cook in batches.
6. Select zone 1, then AIR FRY, then set the temperature to 360 degrees F/ 180 degrees C with a 5-minute timer. To match zone 2 settings to zone 1, choose MATCH. To begin, select START/STOP.
7. Meanwhile, combine all the sauce ingredients together in a bowl.
8. Remove the shrimp when the cooking time is over.

Nutrition Info:

- (Per serving) Calories 415 | Fat 15g | Sodium 1875mg | Carbs 28g | Fiber 1g | Sugar 5g | Protein 38g

Shrimp Skewers

Servings: 4
Cooking Time: 10minutes

Ingredients:

- 453g shrimp
- 15ml lemon juice
- 15ml olive oil
- 1 tbsp old bay seasoning
- 1 tsp garlic, minced

Directions:

1. Toss shrimp with old bay seasoning, garlic, lemon juice, and olive oil in a bowl.
2. Thread shrimp onto the soaked skewers.
3. Insert a crisper plate in the Ninja Foodi air fryer baskets.
4. Place the shrimp skewers in both baskets.
5. Select zone 1, then select "air fry" mode and set the temperature to 390 degrees F for 10 minutes. Press "match" to match zone 2 settings to zone 1. Press "start/stop" to begin.

Nutrition Info:

- (Per serving) Calories 167 | Fat 5.5g |Sodium 758mg | Carbs 2g | Fiber 0g | Sugar 0.1g | Protein 25.9g

Two-way Salmon

Servings:2
Cooking Time:18

Ingredients:

- 2 salmon fillets, 8 ounces each
- 2 tablespoons of Cajun seasoning
- 2 tablespoons of jerk seasoning
- 1 lemon cut in half
- oil spray, for greasing

Directions:

1. First, drizzle lemon juice over the salmon and wash it with tap water.
2. Rinse and pat dry the fillets with a paper towel.
3. Now rub o fillet with Cajun seasoning and grease it with oil spray.
4. Take the second fillet and rub it with jerk seasoning.
5. Grease the second fillet of salmon with oil spray.
6. now put the salmon fillets in both the baskets.
7. Set the Zone 1 basket to 390 degrees F for 16-18 minutes
8. Select MATCH button for zone 2 basket.
9. hit the start button to start cooking.
10. Once the cooking is done, serve the fish hot with mayonnaise.

Nutrition Info:

- (Per serving) Calories 238| Fat 11.8g| Sodium 488mg | Carbs 9g | Fiber 0g | Sugar8 g | Protein 35g

Smoked Salmon

Servings:4
Cooking Time:12

Ingredients:

- 2 pounds of salmon fillets, smoked
- 6 ounces cream cheese
- 4 tablespoons mayonnaise
- 2 teaspoons of chives, fresh
- 1 teaspoon of lemon zest
- Salt and freshly ground black pepper, to taste
- 2 tablespoons of butter

Directions:

1. Cut the salmon into very small and uniform bite-size pieces.
2. Mix cream cheese, chives, mayonnaise, black pepper, and lemon zest, in a small mixing bowl.
3. Let it sit aside for further use.
4. Coat the salmon pieces with salt and butter.
5. Divide the bite-size pieces into both zones of the air fryer.
6. Set it on AIRFRY mode at 400 degrees F for 12 minutes.
7. Select MATCH for zone 2 basket.
8. Hit start, so the cooking start.
9. Once the salmon is done, top it with a bowl creamy mixture and serve.
10. Enjoy hot.

Nutrition Info:

- (Per serving) Calories 557| Fat 15.7 g| Sodium 371mg | Carbs 4.8 g | Fiber 0g | Sugar 1.1g | Protein 48 g

Seafood Shrimp Omelet

Servings:2
Cooking Time:15
Ingredients:

- 6 large shrimp, shells removed and chopped
- 6 eggs, beaten
- ½ tablespoon of butter, melted
- 2 tablespoons green onions, sliced
- 1/3 cup of mushrooms, chopped
- 1 pinch paprika
- Salt and black pepper, to taste
- Oil spray, for greasing

Directions:

1. In a large bowl whisk the eggs and add chopped shrimp, butter, green onions, mushrooms, paprika, salt, and black pepper.
2. Take two cake pans that fit inside the air fryer and grease them with oil spray.
3. Pour the egg mixture between the cake pans and place it in two baskets of the air fryer.
4. Turn on the BAKE function of zone 1, and let it cook for 15 minutes at 320 degrees F.
5. Select the MATCH button to match the cooking time for the zone 2 basket.
6. Once the cooking cycle completes, take out, and serve hot.

Nutrition Info:

- (Per serving) Calories 300 | Fat 17.5g| Sodium 368mg | Carbs 2.9g | Fiber 0.3g | Sugar1.4 g | Protein32.2 g

Fish And Chips

Servings:2
Cooking Time:22
Ingredients:

- 1 pound of potatoes, cut lengthwise
- 1 cup seasoned flour
- 2 eggs, organic
- 1/3 cup buttermilk
- 2 cup seafood fry mix
- ½ cup bread crumbs
- 2 codfish fillet, 6 ounces each
- Oil spray, for greasing

Directions:

1. take a bowl and whisk eggs in it along buttermilk.
2. In a separate bowl mix seafood fry mix and bread crumbs
3. Take a baking tray and spread flour on it
4. Dip the fillets first in egg wash, then in flour, and at the end coat it with breadcrumbs mixture.
5. Put the fish fillet in air fryer zone 1 basket.
6. Grease the fish fillet with oil spray.
7. Set zone 1 to AIR FRY mode at 400 degrees F for 14 minutes.
8. Put potato chip in zone two baskets and lightly grease it with oil spray.
9. Set the zone 2 basket to AIRFRY mode at 400 degrees F for 22 minutes.
10. Hit the smart finish button.
11. Once done, serve and enjoy.

Nutrition Info:

- (Per serving) Calories 992| Fat 22.3g| Sodium1406 mg | Carbs 153.6g | Fiber 10g | Sugar10 g | Protein 40g

Spicy Salmon Fillets

Servings: 6
Cooking Time: 8 Minutes

Ingredients:

- 900g salmon fillets
- ¾ tsp ground cumin
- 1 tbsp brown sugar
- 2 tbsp steak seasoning
- ¼ tsp cayenne pepper
- ½ tsp ground coriander

Directions:

1. Mix ground cumin, coriander, steak seasoning, brown sugar, and cayenne in a small bowl.
2. Rub salmon fillets with spice mixture.
3. Insert a crisper plate in the Ninja Foodi air fryer baskets.
4. Place the salmon fillets in both baskets.
5. Select zone 1, then select "bake" mode and set the temperature to 360 degrees F for 10 minutes. Press "match" to match zone 2 settings to zone 1. Press "start/stop" to begin.

Nutrition Info:

- (Per serving) Calories 207 | Fat 9.4g |Sodium 68mg | Carbs 1.6g | Fiber 0.1g | Sugar 1.5g | Protein 29.4g

Air Fryer Calamari

Servings: 4
Cooking Time: 7 Minutes

Ingredients:

- ½ cup all-purpose flour
- 1 large egg
- 59ml milk
- 2 cups panko bread crumbs
- 1 teaspoon sea salt
- 1 teaspoon black pepper
- 455g calamari rings
- nonstick cooking spray

Directions:

1. Beat egg with milk in a bowl.
2. Mix flour with black pepper and salt in a bowl.
3. Coat the calamari rings with the flour mixture then dip in the egg mixture and coat with the breadcrumbs.
4. Place the coated calamari in the air fryer baskets.
5. Return the air fryer basket 1 to Zone 1, and basket 2 to Zone 2 of the Ninja Foodi 2-Basket Air Fryer.
6. Choose the "Air Fry" mode for Zone 1 at 400 degrees F and 7 minutes of cooking time.
7. Select the "MATCH COOK" option to copy the settings for Zone 2.
8. Initiate cooking by pressing the START/PAUSE BUTTON.
9. Flip the calamari rings once cooked half way through.
10. Serve warm.

Nutrition Info:

- (Per serving) Calories 336 | Fat 6g |Sodium 181mg | Carbs 1.3g | Fiber 0.2g | Sugar 0.4g | Protein 69.2g

Chapter 7 Vegetables And Sides Recipes

Delicious Potatoes & Carrots

Servings: 8
Cooking Time: 25 Minutes

Ingredients:

- 453g carrots, sliced
- 2 tsp smoked paprika
- 21g sugar
- 30ml olive oil
- 453g potatoes, diced
- ¼ tsp thyme
- ½ tsp dried oregano
- 1 tsp garlic powder
- Pepper
- Salt

Directions:

1. In a bowl, toss carrots and potatoes with 1 tablespoon of oil.
2. Insert a crisper plate in the Ninja Foodi air fryer baskets.
3. Add carrots and potatoes to both baskets.
4. Select zone 1 then select "air fry" mode and set the temperature to 390 degrees F for 15 minutes. Press "match" to match zone 2 settings to zone 1. Press "start/stop" to begin.
5. In a mixing bowl, add cooked potatoes, carrots, smoked paprika, sugar, oil, thyme, oregano, garlic powder, pepper, and salt and toss well.
6. Return carrot and potato mixture into the air fryer basket and cook for 10 minutes more.

Nutrition Info:

- (Per serving) Calories 101 | Fat 3.6g |Sodium 62mg | Carbs 16.6g | Fiber 3g | Sugar 5.1g | Protein 1.6g

Curly Fries

Servings: 6
Cooking Time: 20 Minutes.

Ingredients:

- 2 spiralized zucchinis
- 1 cup flour
- 2 tablespoons paprika
- 1 teaspoon cayenne pepper
- 1 teaspoon garlic powder
-
- 1 teaspoon black pepper
- 1 teaspoon salt
- 2 eggs
- Olive oil or cooking spray

Directions:

1. Mix flour with paprika, cayenne pepper, garlic powder, black pepper, and salt in a bowl.
2. Beat eggs in another bowl and dip the zucchini in the eggs.
3. Coat the zucchini with the flour mixture and divide it into two crisper plates.
4. Spray the zucchini with cooking oil.
5. Return the crisper plate to the Ninja Foodi Dual Zone Air Fryer.
6. Choose the Air Fry mode for Zone 1 and set the temperature to 400 degrees F and the time to 20 minutes.
7. Select the "MATCH" button to copy the settings for Zone 2.
8. Initiate cooking by pressing the START/STOP button.
9. Toss the zucchini once cooked halfway through, then resume cooking.
10. Serve warm.

Nutrition Info:

- (Per serving) Calories 212 | Fat 11.8g |Sodium 321mg | Carbs 24.6g | Fiber 4.4g | Sugar 8g | Protein 7.3g

Jerk Tofu With Roasted Cabbage

Servings:4
Cooking Time: 20 Minutes

Ingredients:

- FOR THE JERK TOFU
- 1 (14-ounce) package extra-firm tofu, drained
- 1 tablespoon apple cider vinegar
- 1 tablespoon reduced-sodium soy sauce
- 2 tablespoons jerk seasoning
- Juice of 1 lime
- ½ teaspoon kosher salt
- 2 tablespoons olive oil
- FOR THE CABBAGE
- 1 (14-ounce) bag coleslaw mix
- 1 red bell pepper, thinly sliced
- 2 scallions, thinly sliced
- 2 tablespoons water
- 3 garlic cloves, minced
- ¼ teaspoon fresh thyme leaves
- ¼ teaspoon onion powder
- ¼ teaspoon kosher salt
- ¼ teaspoon freshly ground black pepper

Directions:

1. To prep the jerk tofu: Cut the tofu horizontally into 4 slabs.
2. In a shallow dish (big enough to hold the tofu slabs), whisk together the vinegar, soy sauce, jerk seasoning, lime juice, and salt.
3. Place the tofu in the marinade and turn to coat both sides. Cover and marinate for at least 15 minutes (or up to overnight in the refrigerator).
4. To prep the cabbage: In the Zone 2 basket, combine the coleslaw, bell pepper, scallions, water, garlic, thyme, onion powder, salt, and black pepper.
5. To cook the tofu and cabbage: Install a crisper plate in the Zone 1 basket and add the tofu in a single layer. Brush the tofu with the oil and insert the basket in the unit. Insert the Zone 2 basket in the unit.
6. Select Zone 1, select AIR FRY, set the temperature to 390°F, and set the timer to 15 minutes.
7. Select Zone 2, select ROAST, set the temperature to 330°F, and set the timer to 20 minutes. Select SMART FINISH.
8. Press START/PAUSE to begin cooking.
9. When both timers read 5 minutes, press START/PAUSE. Remove the Zone 1 basket and use silicone-tipped tongs to flip the tofu. Reinsert the basket in the unit. Remove the Zone 2 basket and stir the cabbage. Reinsert the basket and press START/PAUSE to resume cooking.
10. When cooking is complete, the tofu will be crispy and browned around the edges and the cabbage soft.
11. Transfer the tofu to four plates and serve with the cabbage on the side.

Nutrition Info:

- (Per serving) Calories: 220; Total fat: 12g; Saturated fat: 1.5g; Carbohydrates: 21g; Fiber: 5g; Protein: 12g; Sodium: 817mg

Garlic-herb Fried Squash

Servings: 4
Cooking Time: 15 Minutes
Ingredients:

- 5 cups halved small pattypan squash (about 1¼ pounds)
- 1 tablespoon olive oil
- 2 garlic cloves, minced
- ½ teaspoon salt
- ¼ teaspoon dried oregano
- ¼ teaspoon dried thyme
- ¼ teaspoon pepper
- 1 tablespoon minced fresh parsley, for serving

Directions:

1. Place the squash in a large bowl.
2. Mix the oil, garlic, salt, oregano, thyme, and pepper; drizzle over the squash. Toss to coat.
3. Place a crisper plate in both drawers. Put the squash in a single layer in each drawer. Insert the drawers into the unit.
4. Select zone 1, then AIR FRY, then set the temperature to 360 degrees F/ 180 degrees C with a 6-minute timer. To match zone 2 settings to zone 1, choose MATCH. To begin, select START/STOP.
5. Remove the squash from the drawers after the timer has finished. Sprinkle with the parsley.

Nutrition Info:

- (Per serving) Calories 58 | Fat 3g | Sodium 296mg | Carbs 6g | Fiber 2g | Sugar 3g | Protein 2g

Rosemary Asparagus & Potatoes

Servings: 6
Cooking Time: 30 Minutes
Ingredients:

- 125g asparagus, trimmed & cut into pieces
- 2 tsp garlic powder
- 2 tbsp rosemary, chopped
- 30ml olive oil
- 679g baby potatoes, quartered
- ½ tsp red pepper flakes
- Pepper
- Salt

Directions:

1. Insert a crisper plate in the Ninja Foodi air fryer baskets.
2. Toss potatoes with 1 tablespoon of oil, pepper, and salt in a bowl until well coated.
3. Add potatoes into in zone 1 basket.
4. Toss asparagus with remaining oil, red pepper flakes, pepper, garlic powder, and rosemary in a mixing bowl.
5. Add asparagus into the zone 2 basket.
6. Select zone 1, then select "air fry" mode and set the temperature to 390 degrees F for 20 minutes. Select zone 2, then select "air fry" mode and set the temperature to 390 degrees F for 10 minutes. Press "match" mode, then press "start/stop" to begin.

Nutrition Info:

- (Per serving) Calories 121 | Fat 5g |Sodium 40mg | Carbs 17.1g | Fiber 4.2g | Sugar 1g | Protein 4g

Cheesy Potatoes With Asparagus

Servings:2
Cooking Time:35
Ingredients:

- 1-1/2 pounds of russet potato, wedges or cut in half
- 2 teaspoons mixed herbs
- 2 teaspoons chili flakes
- 2 cups asparagus
- 1 cup chopped onion
- 1 tablespoon Dijon mustard
-
- 1/4 cup fresh cream
- 1 teaspoon olive oil
- 2 tablespoons of butter
- 1/2 teaspoon salt and black pepper
- Water as required
- 1/2 cup Parmesan cheese

Directions:

1. Take a bowl and add asparagus and sweet potato wedges to it.
2. Season it with salt, black pepper, and olive oil.
3. Now add the potato wedges to the zone 1 air fryer basket and asparagus to the zone 2 basket.
4. Set basket1 to AIRFRY mode at 390 degrees F for 12 minutes.
5. Set the zone 2 basket at 390 degrees F, for 30-35 minutes.
6. Meanwhile, take a skillet and add butter and sauté onion in it for a few minutes.
7. Then add salt and Dijon mustard and chili flakes, Parmesan cheese, and fresh cream.
8. Once the air fry mode is done, take out the potato and asparagus.
9. Drizzle the skillet ingredients over the potatoes and serve with asparagus.

Nutrition Info:

- (Per serving) Calories 251| Fat11g | Sodium 279mg | Carbs 31.1g | Fiber 5g | Sugar 4.1g | Protein9 g

Sweet Potatoes With Honey Butter

Servings: 4
Cooking Time: 40 Minutes.
Ingredients:

- 4 sweet potatoes, scrubbed
- 1 teaspoon oil
- Honey Butter
- 4 tablespoons unsalted butter
- 1 tablespoon Honey
- 2 teaspoons hot sauce
- ¼ teaspoon salt

Directions:

1. Rub the sweet potatoes with oil and place two potatoes in each crisper plate.
2. Return the crisper plate to the Ninja Foodi Dual Zone Air Fryer.
3. Choose the Air Fry mode for Zone 1 and set the temperature to 400 degrees F and the time to 40 minutes.
4. Select the "MATCH" button to copy the settings for Zone 2.
5. Initiate cooking by pressing the START/STOP button.
6. Flip the potatoes once cooked halfway through, then resume cooking.
7. Mix butter with hot sauce, honey, and salt in a bowl.
8. When the potatoes are done, cut a slit on top and make a well with a spoon
9. Pour the honey butter in each potato jacket.
10. Serve.

Nutrition Info:

- (Per serving) Calories 288 | Fat 6.9g |Sodium 761mg | Carbs 46g | Fiber 4g | Sugar 12g | Protein 9.6g

Green Beans With Baked Potatoes

Servings:2
Cooking Time:45

Ingredients:

- 2 cups of green beans
- 2 large potatoes, cubed
- 3 tablespoons of olive oil
- 1 teaspoon of seasoned salt
-
- ½ teaspoon chili powder
- 1/6 teaspoon garlic powder
- 1/4 teaspoon onion powder

Directions:

1. Take a large bowl and pour olive oil into it.
2. Now add all the seasoning in the olive oil and whisk it well.
3. Toss the green bean in it, then transfer it to zone 1 basket of the air fryer.
4. Now season the potatoes with the seasoning and add them to the zone 2 basket.
5. Now set the zone one basket to AIRFRY mode at 350 degrees F for 18 minutes.
6. Now hit 2 for the second basket and set it to AIR FRY mode at 350 degrees F, for 45 minutes.
7. Once the cooking cycle is complete, take out and serve it by transferring it to the serving plates.

Nutrition Info:

- (Per serving) Calories473 | Fat21.6g | Sodium796 mg | Carbs 66.6g | Fiber12.9 g | Sugar6 g | Protein8.4 g

Beets With Orange Gremolata And Goat's Cheese

Servings: 12
Cooking Time: 45 Minutes

Ingredients:

- 3 medium fresh golden beets (about 1 pound)
- 3 medium fresh beets (about 1 pound)
- 2 tablespoons lime juice
- 2 tablespoons orange juice
- ½ teaspoon fine sea salt
- 1 tablespoon minced fresh parsley
- 1 tablespoon minced fresh sage
- 1 garlic clove, minced
- 1 teaspoon grated orange zest
- 3 tablespoons crumbled goat's cheese
- 2 tablespoons sunflower kernels

Directions:

1. Scrub the beets and trim the tops by 1 inch.
2. Place the beets on a double thickness of heavy-duty foil (about 24 x 12 inches). Fold the foil around the beets, sealing tightly.
3. Place a crisper plate in both drawers. Put the beets in a single layer in each drawer. Insert the drawers into the unit.
4. Select zone 1, then AIR FRY, then set the temperature to 360 degrees F/ 180 degrees C with a 45-minute timer. To match zone 2 settings to zone 1, choose MATCH. To begin, select START/STOP.
5. Remove the beets from the drawers after the timer has finished. Peel, halve, and slice them when they're cool enough to handle. Place them in a serving bowl.
6. Toss in the lime juice, orange juice, and salt to coat. Sprinkle the beets with the parsley, sage, garlic, and orange zest. The sunflower kernels and goat's cheese go on top.

Nutrition Info:

- (Per serving) Calories 481 | Fat 20g | Sodium 1162mg | Carbs 56g | Fiber 4g | Sugar 9g | Protein 19g

Buffalo Seitan With Crispy Zucchini Noodles

Servings:4
Cooking Time: 12 Minutes
Ingredients:

- FOR THE BUFFALO SEITAN
- 1 (8-ounce) package precooked seitan strips
- 1 teaspoon garlic powder, divided
- ½ teaspoon onion powder
- ¼ teaspoon smoked paprika
- ¼ cup Louisiana-style hot sauce
- 2 tablespoons vegetable oil
- 1 tablespoon tomato paste
- ¼ teaspoon freshly ground black pepper
- FOR THE ZUCCHINI NOODLES
- 3 large egg whites
- 1¼ cups all-purpose flour
- 1 teaspoon kosher salt, divided
- 12 ounces seltzer water or club soda
- 5 ounces zucchini noodles
- Nonstick cooking spray

Directions:

1. To prep the Buffalo seitan: Season the seitan strips with ½ teaspoon of garlic powder, the onion powder, and smoked paprika.
2. In a large bowl, whisk together the hot sauce, oil, tomato paste, remaining ½ teaspoon of garlic powder, and the black pepper. Set the bowl of Buffalo sauce aside.
3. To prep the zucchini noodles: In a medium bowl, use a handheld mixer to beat the egg whites until stiff peaks form.
4. In a large bowl, combine the flour and ½ teaspoon of salt. Mix in the seltzer to form a thin batter. Fold in the beaten egg whites.
5. Add the zucchini to the batter and gently mix to coat.
6. To cook the seitan and zucchini noodles: Install a crisper plate in each of the two baskets. Place the seitan in the Zone 1 basket and insert the basket in the unit. Lift the noodles from the batter one at a time, letting the excess drip off, and place them in the Zone 2 basket. Insert the basket in the unit.
7. Select Zone 1, select BAKE, set the temperature to 370°F, and set the timer to 12 minutes.
8. Select Zone 2, select AIR FRY, set the temperature to 400°F, and set the timer to 12 minutes. Select SMART FINISH.
9. Press START/PAUSE to begin cooking.
10. When the Zone 1 timer reads 2 minutes, press START/PAUSE. Remove the basket and transfer the seitan to the bowl of Buffalo sauce. Turn to coat, then return the seitan to the basket. Reinsert the basket and press START/PAUSE to resume cooking.
11. When cooking is complete, the seitan should be warmed through and the zucchini noodles crisp and light golden brown.
12. Sprinkle the zucchini noodles with the remaining ½ teaspoon of salt. If desired, drizzle extra Buffalo sauce over the seitan. Serve hot.

Nutrition Info:

- (Per serving) Calories: 252; Total fat: 15g; Saturated fat: 1g; Carbohydrates: 22g; Fiber: 1.5g; Protein: 13g; Sodium: 740mg

Fried Avocado Tacos

Servings: 4
Cooking Time: 10 Minutes

Ingredients:

- For the sauce:
- 2 cups shredded fresh kale or coleslaw mix
- ¼ cup minced fresh cilantro
- ¼ cup plain Greek yogurt
- 2 tablespoons lime juice
- 1 teaspoon honey
- ¼ teaspoon salt
- ¼ teaspoon ground chipotle pepper
- ¼ teaspoon pepper
- For the tacos:
- 1 large egg, beaten
- ¼ cup cornmeal
- ½ teaspoon salt
- ½ teaspoon garlic powder
- ½ teaspoon ground chipotle pepper
- 2 medium avocados, peeled and sliced
- Cooking spray
- 8 flour tortillas or corn tortillas (6 inches), heated up
- 1 medium tomato, chopped
- Crumbled queso fresco (optional)

Directions:

1. Combine the first 8 ingredients in a bowl. Cover and refrigerate until serving.
2. Place the egg in a shallow bowl. In another shallow bowl, mix the cornmeal, salt, garlic powder, and chipotle pepper.
3. Dip the avocado slices in the egg, then into the cornmeal mixture, gently patting to help adhere.
4. Place a crisper plate in both drawers. Put the avocado slices in the drawers in a single layer. Insert the drawers into the unit.
5. Select zone 1, then AIR FRY, then set the temperature to 360 degrees F/ 180 degrees C with a 6-minute timer. To match zone 2 settings to zone 1, choose MATCH. To begin, select START/STOP.
6. Put the avocado slices, prepared sauce, tomato, and queso fresco in the tortillas and serve.

Nutrition Info:

- (Per serving) Calories 407 | Fat 21g | Sodium 738mg | Carbs 48g | Fiber 4g | Sugar 9g | Protein 9g

Quinoa Patties

Servings: 4
Cooking Time: 32 Minutes.

Ingredients:

- 1 cup quinoa red
- 1½ cups water
- 1 teaspoon salt
- black pepper, ground
- 1½ cups rolled oats
- 3 eggs beaten
- ¼ cup minced white onion
- ½ cup crumbled feta cheese
- ¼ cup chopped fresh chives
- Salt and black pepper, to taste
- Vegetable or canola oil
- 4 hamburger buns
- 4 arugulas
- 4 slices tomato sliced
- Cucumber yogurt dill sauce
- 1 cup cucumber, diced
- 1 cup Greek yogurt
- 2 teaspoons lemon juice
- ¼ teaspoon salt
- Black pepper, ground
- 1 tablespoon chopped fresh dill
- 1 tablespoon olive oil

Directions:

1. Add quinoa to a saucepan filled with cold water, salt, and black pepper, and place it over medium-high heat.
2. Cook the quinoa to a boil, then reduce the heat, cover, and cook for 20 minutes on a simmer.
3. Fluff and mix the cooked quinoa with a fork and remove it from the heat.
4. Spread the quinoa in a baking stay.
5. Mix eggs, oats, onion, herbs, cheese, salt, and black pepper.
6. Stir in quinoa, then mix well. Make 4 patties out of this quinoa cheese mixture.
7. Divide the patties in the two crisper plates and spray them with cooking oil.
8. Return the crisper plates to the Ninja Foodi Dual Zone Air Fryer.
9. Choose the Air Fry mode for Zone 1 and set the temperature to 390 degrees F and the time to 13 minutes.
10. Select the "MATCH" button to copy the settings for Zone 2.
11. Initiate cooking by pressing the START/STOP button.
12. Flip the patties once cooked halfway through, and resume cooking.
13. Meanwhile, prepare the cucumber yogurt dill sauce by mixing all of its ingredients in a mixing bowl.
14. Place each quinoa patty in a burger bun along with arugula leaves.
15. Serve with yogurt dill sauce.

Nutrition Info:

- (Per serving) Calories 231 | Fat 9g |Sodium 271mg | Carbs 32.8g | Fiber 6.4g | Sugar 7g | Protein 6.3g

Veggie Burgers With "fried" Onion Rings

Servings:4
Cooking Time: 25 Minutes

Ingredients:

- FOR THE VEGGIE BURGERS
- 1 (15-ounce) can black beans, drained and rinsed
- ½ cup panko bread crumbs
- 1 large egg
- ¼ cup finely chopped red bell pepper
- ¼ cup frozen corn, thawed
- 1 tablespoon olive oil
- ½ teaspoon garlic powder
- ½ teaspoon ground cumin
- ¼ teaspoon smoked paprika
- Nonstick cooking spray
- 4 hamburger buns
- ¼ cup barbecue sauce, for serving
- FOR THE ONION RINGS
- 1 large sweet onion
- ½ cup all-purpose flour
- 2 large eggs
- 1 cup panko bread crumbs
- ½ teaspoon kosher salt
- Nonstick cooking spray

Directions:

1. To prep the veggie burgers: In a large bowl, mash the beans with a potato masher or a fork. Stir in the panko, egg, bell pepper, corn, oil, garlic powder, cumin, and smoked paprika. Mix well.
2. Shape the mixture into 4 patties. Spritz both sides of each patty with cooking spray.
3. To prep the onion rings: Cut the onion into ½-inch-thick rings.
4. Set up a breading station with three small shallow bowls. Place the flour in the first bowl. In the second bowl, beat the eggs. Place the panko and salt in the third bowl.
5. Bread the onions rings in this order: First, dip them into the flour, coating both sides. Then, dip into the beaten egg. Finally, coat them in the panko. Spritz each with cooking spray.
6. To cook the burgers and onion rings: Install a crisper plate in each of the two baskets. Place 2 veggie burgers in the Zone 1 basket. Place the onion rings in the Zone 2 basket and insert both baskets in the unit.
7. Select Zone 1, select AIR FRY, set the temperature to 390°F, and set the timer to 25 minutes.
8. Select Zone 2, select AIR FRY, set the temperature to 375°F, and set the timer to 10 minutes. Select SMART FINISH.
9. Press START/PAUSE to begin cooking.
10. When the Zone 1 timer reads 10 minutes, press START/PAUSE. Remove the basket and use a silicone spatula to flip the burgers. Reinsert the basket and press START/PAUSE to resume cooking.
11. When the Zone 1 timer reads 10 minutes, press START/PAUSE. Remove the basket and transfer the burgers to a plate. Place the 2 remaining burgers in the basket. Reinsert the basket and press START/PAUSE to resume cooking.
12. When both timers read 5 minutes, press START/PAUSE. Remove the Zone 1 basket and flip the burgers, then reinsert the basket. Remove the Zone 2 basket and shake vigorously to rearrange the onion rings and separate any that have stuck together. Reinsert the basket and press START/PAUSE to resume cooking.
13. When cooking is complete, the veggie burgers should be cooked through and the onion rings golden brown.
14. Place 1 burger on each bun. Top with barbecue sauce and serve with onion rings on the side.

Nutrition Info:

- (Per serving) Calories: 538; Total fat: 16g; Saturated fat: 2g; Carbohydrates: 83g; Fiber: 10g; Protein: 19g; Sodium: 914mg

Acorn Squash Slices

Servings: 6
Cooking Time: 10 Minutes

Ingredients:

- 2 medium acorn squashes
- ⅔ cup packed brown sugar
- ½ cup butter, melted

Directions:

1. Cut the squash in half, remove the seeds and slice into ½ inch slices.
2. Place the squash slices in the air fryer baskets.
3. Drizzle brown sugar and butter over the squash slices.
4. Return the air fryer basket 1 to Zone 1, and basket 2 to Zone 2 of the Ninja Foodi 2-Basket Air Fryer.
5. Choose the "Air Fry" mode for Zone 1 and set the temperature to 350 degrees F and 10 minutes of cooking time.
6. Select the "MATCH COOK" option to copy the settings for Zone 2.
7. Initiate cooking by pressing the START/PAUSE BUTTON.
8. Flip the squash once cooked halfway through.
9. Serve.

Nutrition Info:

- (Per serving) Calories 206 | Fat 3.4g |Sodium 174mg | Carbs 35g | Fiber 9.4g | Sugar 5.9g | Protein 10.6g

Stuffed Sweet Potatoes

Servings: 4
Cooking Time: 55 Minutes

Ingredients:

- 2 medium sweet potatoes
- 1 teaspoon olive oil
- 1 cup cooked chopped spinach, drained
- 1 cup shredded cheddar cheese, divided
- 2 cooked bacon strips, crumbled
- 1 green onion, chopped
- ¼ cup fresh cranberries, coarsely chopped
- 1/3 cup chopped pecans, toasted
- 2 tablespoons butter
- ¼ teaspoon kosher salt
- ¼ teaspoon pepper

Directions:

1. Brush the sweet potatoes with the oil.
2. Place a crisper plate in both drawers. Add one sweet potato to each drawer. Place the drawers in the unit.
3. Select zone 1, then AIR FRY, then set the temperature to 360 degrees F/ 180 degrees C with a 40-minute timer. To match zone 2 settings to zone 1, choose MATCH. To begin, select START/STOP.
4. Remove the sweet potatoes from the drawers after the timer has finished. Cut them in half lengthwise. Scoop out the pulp, leaving a ¼-inch thick shell.
5. Put the pulp in a large bowl and stir in the spinach, ¾ cup of cheese, bacon, onion, pecans, cranberries, butter, salt, and pepper.
6. Spoon the mixture into the potato shells, mounding the mixture slightly.
7. Place a crisper plate in each drawer. Put one filled potato into each drawer and insert them into the unit.
8. Select zone 1, then AIR FRY, then set the temperature to 360 degrees F/ 180 degrees C with a 10-minute timer. To match zone 2 settings to zone 1, choose MATCH. To begin, select START/STOP.
9. Sprinkle with the remaining ¼ cup of cheese. Cook using the same settings until the cheese is melted (about 1 to 2 minutes).

Nutrition Info:

- (Per serving) Calories 376 | Fat 25g | Sodium 489mg | Carbs 28g | Fiber 10g | Sugar 5g | Protein 12g

Air Fryer Vegetables

Servings: 2
Cooking Time: 15 Minutes
Ingredients:

- 1 courgette, diced
- 2 capsicums, diced
- 1 head broccoli, diced
- 1 red onion, diced
- Marinade
- 1 teaspoon smoked paprika
- 1 teaspoon garlic granules
- 1 teaspoon Herb de Provence
- Salt and black pepper, to taste
- 1½ tablespoon olive oil
- 2 tablespoons lemon juice

Directions:

1. Toss the veggies with the rest of the marinade ingredients in a bowl.
2. Spread the veggies in the air fryer baskets.
3. Return the air fryer basket 1 to Zone 1, and basket 2 to Zone 2 of the Ninja Foodi 2-Basket Air Fryer.
4. Choose the "Air Fry" mode for Zone 1 at 400 degrees F and 15 minutes of cooking time.
5. Select the "MATCH COOK" option to copy the settings for Zone 2.
6. Initiate cooking by pressing the START/PAUSE BUTTON.
7. Toss the veggies once cooked half way through.
8. Serve warm.

Nutrition Info:

- (Per serving) Calories 166 | Fat 3.2g |Sodium 437mg | Carbs 28.8g | Fiber 1.8g | Sugar 2.7g | Protein 5.8g

Balsamic Vegetables

Servings: 4
Cooking Time: 13 Minutes
Ingredients:

- 125g asparagus, cut woody ends
- 88g mushrooms, halved
- 1 tbsp Dijon mustard
- 3 tbsp soy sauce
- 27g brown sugar
- 57ml balsamic vinegar
-
- 32g olive oil
- 1 zucchini, sliced
- 1 yellow squash, sliced
- 170g grape tomatoes
- Pepper
- Salt

Directions:

1. In a bowl, mix asparagus, tomatoes, oil, mustard, soy sauce, mushrooms, zucchini, squash, brown sugar, vinegar, pepper, and salt.
2. Cover the bowl and place it in the refrigerator for 45 minutes.
3. Insert a crisper plate in the Ninja Foodi air fryer baskets.
4. Add the vegetable mixture in both baskets.
5. Select zone 1, then select "air fry" mode and set the temperature to 390 degrees F for 12 minutes. Press "match" to match zone 2 settings to zone 1. Press "start/stop" to begin. Stir halfway through.

Nutrition Info:

- (Per serving) Calories 184 | Fat 13.3g |Sodium 778mg | Carbs 14.7g | Fiber 3.6g | Sugar 9.5g | Protein 5.5g

Hasselback Potatoes

Servings: 4
Cooking Time: 15 Minutes.

Ingredients:

- 4 medium Yukon Gold potatoes
- 3 tablespoons melted butter
- 1 tablespoon olive oil
- 3 garlic cloves, crushed
- ½ teaspoon ground paprika
- Salt and black pepper ground, to taste
- 1 tablespoon chopped fresh parsley

Directions:

1. Slice each potato from the top to make ¼-inch slices without cutting its ½-inch bottom, keeping the potato's bottom intact.
2. Mix butter with olive oil, garlic, and paprika in a small bowl.
3. Brush the garlic mixture on top of each potato and add the mixture into the slits.
4. Season them with salt and black pepper.
5. Place 2 seasoned potatoes in each of the crisper plate
6. Return the crisper plate to the Ninja Foodi Dual Zone Air Fryer.
7. Choose the Air Fry mode for Zone 1 and set the temperature to 375 degrees F and the time to 25 minutes.
8. Select the "MATCH" button to copy the settings for Zone 2.
9. Initiate cooking by pressing the START/STOP button.
10. Brushing the potatoes again with butter mixture after 15 minutes, then resume cooking.
11. Garnish with parsley.
12. Serve warm.

Nutrition Info:

- (Per serving) Calories 350 | Fat 2.6g |Sodium 358mg | Carbs 64.6g | Fiber 14.4g | Sugar 3.3g | Protein 19.9g

Bbq Corn

Servings: 4
Cooking Time: 10 Minutes

Ingredients:

- 450g can baby corn, drained & rinsed
- 56g BBQ sauce
- ½ tsp Sriracha sauce

Directions:

1. In a bowl, toss the baby corn with sriracha sauce and BBQ sauce until well coated.
2. Insert a crisper plate in the Ninja Foodi air fryer baskets.
3. Add the baby corn to both baskets.
4. Select zone 1, then select "air fry" mode and set the temperature to 390 degrees F for 10 minutes. Press "match" to match zone 2 settings to zone 1. Press "start/stop" to begin. Stir halfway through.

Nutrition Info:

- (Per serving) Calories 46 | Fat 0.1g |Sodium 446mg | Carbs 10.2g | Fiber 2.8g | Sugar 5.9g | Protein 0.9g

Balsamic-glazed Tofu With Roasted Butternut Squash

Servings:4
Cooking Time: 40 Minutes

Ingredients:

- FOR THE BALSAMIC TOFU
- 2 tablespoons balsamic vinegar
- 1 tablespoon maple syrup
- 1 teaspoon soy sauce
- 1 teaspoon Dijon mustard
- 1 (14-ounce) package firm tofu, drained and cut into large cubes
- 1 tablespoon canola oil
- FOR THE BUTTERNUT SQUASH
- 1 small butternut squash
- 1 tablespoon canola oil
- 1 teaspoon light brown sugar
- ¼ teaspoon kosher salt
- ¼ teaspoon freshly ground black pepper
-

Directions:

1. To prep the balsamic tofu: In a large bowl, whisk together the vinegar, maple syrup, soy sauce, and mustard. Add the tofu and stir to coat. Cover and marinate for at least 20 minutes (or up to overnight in the refrigerator).
2. To prep the butternut squash: Peel the squash and cut in half lengthwise. Remove and discard the seeds. Cut the squash crosswise into ½-inch-thick slices.
3. Brush the squash pieces with the oil, then sprinkle with the brown sugar, salt, and black pepper.
4. To cook the tofu and squash: Install a crisper plate in each of the two baskets. Place the tofu in the Zone 1 basket, drizzle with the oil, and insert the basket in the unit. Place the squash in the Zone 2 basket and insert the basket in the unit.
5. Select Zone 1, select AIR FRY, set the temperature to 400°F, and set the timer to 10 minutes.
6. Select Zone 2, select ROAST, set the temperature to 400°F, and set the timer to 40 minutes. Select SMART FINISH.
7. Press START/PAUSE to begin cooking.
8. When cooking is complete, the tofu will have begun to crisp and brown around the edges and the squash should be tender. Serve hot.

Nutrition Info:

- (Per serving) Calories: 253; Total fat: 11g; Saturated fat: 1g; Carbohydrates: 30g; Fiber: 4.5g; Protein: 11g; Sodium: 237mg

Fried Olives

Servings: 6
Cooking Time: 9 Minutes.

Ingredients:

- 2 cups blue cheese stuffed olives, drained
- ½ cup all-purpose flour
- 1 cup panko breadcrumbs
- ½ teaspoon garlic powder
- 1 pinch oregano
- 2 eggs
-

Directions:

1. Mix flour with oregano and garlic powder in a bowl and beat two eggs in another bowl.
2. Spread panko breadcrumbs in a bowl.
3. Coat all the olives with the flour mixture, dip in the eggs and then coat with the panko breadcrumbs.
4. As you coat the olives, place them in the two crisper plates in a single layer, then spray them with cooking oil.
5. Return the crisper plates to the Ninja Foodi Dual Zone Air Fryer.
6. Choose the Air Fry mode for Zone 1 and set the temperature to 375 degrees F and the time to 9 minutes.
7. Select the "MATCH" button to copy the settings for Zone 2.
8. Initiate cooking by pressing the START/STOP button.
9. Flip the olives once cooked halfway through, then resume cooking.
10. Serve.

Nutrition Info:

- (Per serving) Calories 166 | Fat 3.2g |Sodium 437mg | Carbs 28.8g | Fiber 1.8g | Sugar 2.7g | Protein 5.8g

Flavourful Mexican Cauliflower

Servings: 4
Cooking Time: 12 Minutes

Ingredients:

- 1 medium cauliflower head, cut into florets
- ½ tsp turmeric
- 1 tsp onion powder
- 2 tsp garlic powder
- 2 tsp parsley
- 1 lime juice
- 30ml olive oil
- 1 tsp chilli powder
- 1 tsp cumin
- Pepper
- Salt

Directions:

1. In a bowl, toss cauliflower florets with onion powder, garlic powder, parsley, oil, chilli powder, turmeric, cumin, pepper, and salt.
2. Insert a crisper plate in the Ninja Foodi air fryer baskets.
3. Add cauliflower florets in both baskets.
4. Select zone 1, then select "air fry" mode and set the temperature to 390 degrees F for 12 minutes. Press "match" to match zone 2 settings to zone 1. Press "start/stop" to begin. Stir halfway through.
5. Drizzle lime juice over cauliflower florets.

Nutrition Info:

- (Per serving) Calories 108 | Fat 7.4g |Sodium 91mg | Carbs 10g | Fiber 4.1g | Sugar 4.1g | Protein 3.4g

Brussels Sprouts

Servings:2
Cooking Time:20

Ingredients:

- 2 pounds Brussels sprouts
- 2 tablespoons avocado oil
- Salt and pepper, to taste
- 1 cup pine nuts, roasted

Directions:

1. Trim the bottom of Brussels sprouts.
2. Take a bowl and combine the avocado oil, salt, and black pepper.
3. Toss the Brussels sprouts well.
4. Divide it in both air fryer baskets.
5. For the zone 1 basket use AIR fry mode for 20 minutes at 390 degrees F.
6. Select the MATCH button for the zone 2 basket.
7. Once the Brussels sprouts get crisp and tender, take out and serve.

Nutrition Info:

- (Per serving) Calories 672| Fat 50g| Sodium 115mg | Carbs 51g | Fiber 20.2g | Sugar 12.3g | Protein 25g

Caprese Panini With Zucchini Chips

Servings:4
Cooking Time: 20 Minutes

Ingredients:

- FOR THE PANINI
- 4 tablespoons pesto
- 8 slices Italian-style sandwich bread
- 1 tomato, diced
- 6 ounces fresh mozzarella cheese, shredded
- ¼ cup mayonnaise
- FOR THE ZUCCHINI CHIPS
- ½ cup all-purpose flour
- 2 large eggs
- ¼ teaspoon freshly ground black pepper
- ⅛ teaspoon kosher salt
- ½ cup panko bread crumbs
- ¼ cup grated Parmesan cheese
- 1 teaspoon Italian seasoning
- 1 medium zucchini, cut into ¼-inch-thick rounds
- 2 tablespoons vegetable oil

Directions:

1. To prep the panini: Spread 1 tablespoon of pesto each on 4 slices of the bread. Layer the diced tomato and shredded mozzarella on the other 4 slices of bread. Top the tomato/cheese mixture with the pesto-coated bread, pesto-side down, to form 4 sandwiches.
2. Spread the outside of each sandwich (both bread slices) with a thin layer of the mayonnaise.
3. To prep the zucchini chips: Set up a breading station with three small shallow bowls. Place the flour in the first bowl. In the second bowl, beat together the eggs, salt, and black pepper. Place the panko, Parmesan, and Italian seasoning in the third bowl.
4. Bread the zucchini in this order: First, dip the slices into the flour, coating both sides. Then, dip into the beaten egg. Finally, coat in the panko mixture. Drizzle the zucchini on both sides with the oil.
5. To cook the panini and zucchini chips: Install a crisper plate in each of the two baskets. Place 2 sandwiches in the Zone 1 basket and insert the basket in the unit. Place half of the zucchini chips in a single layer in the Zone 2 basket and insert the basket in the unit.
6. Select Zone 1, select AIR FRY, set the temperature to 375°F, and set the timer to 20 minutes.
7. Select Zone 2, select AIR FRY, set the temperature to 400°F, and set the timer to 20 minutes. Select SMART FINISH.
8. Press START/PAUSE to begin cooking.
9. When the Zone 1 timer reads 15 minutes, press START/PAUSE. Remove the basket, and use silicone-tipped tongs or a spatula to flip the sandwiches. Reinsert the basket and press START/PAUSE to resume cooking.
10. When both timers read 10 minutes, press START/PAUSE. Remove the Zone 1 basket and transfer the sandwiches to a plate. Place the remaining 2 sandwiches into the basket and insert the basket in the unit. Remove the Zone 2 basket and transfer the zucchini chips to a serving plate. Place the remaining zucchini chips in the basket. Reinsert the basket and press START/PAUSE to resume cooking.
11. When the Zone 1 timer reads 5 minutes, press START/PAUSE. Remove the basket and flip the sandwiches. Reinsert the basket and press START/PAUSE to resume cooking.
12. When cooking is complete, the panini should be toasted and the zucchini chips golden brown and crisp.
13. Cut each panini in half. Serve hot with zucchini chips on the side.

Nutrition Info:

- (Per serving) Calories: 751; Total fat: 39g; Saturated fat: 9.5g; Carbohydrates: 77g; Fiber: 3.5g; Protein: 23g; Sodium: 1,086mg

Air Fried Okra

Servings: 2
Cooking Time: 13 Minutes.

Ingredients:

- ½ lb. okra pods sliced
- 1 teaspoon olive oil
- ¼ teaspoon salt
- ⅛ teaspoon black pepper

Directions:

1. Preheat the Ninja Foodi Dual Zone Air Fryer to 350 degrees F.
2. Toss okra with olive oil, salt, and black pepper in a bowl.
3. Spread the okra in a single layer in the two crisper plates.
4. Return the crisper plate to the Ninja Foodi Dual Zone Air Fryer.
5. Choose the Air Fry mode for Zone 1 and set the temperature to 375 degrees F and the time to 13 minutes.
6. Select the "MATCH" button to copy the settings for Zone 2.
7. Initiate cooking by pressing the START/STOP button.
8. Toss the okra once cooked halfway through, and resume cooking.
9. Serve warm.

Nutrition Info:

- (Per serving) Calories 208 | Fat 5g |Sodium 1205mg | Carbs 34.1g | Fiber 7.8g | Sugar 2.5g | Protein 5.9g

Chapter 8 Desserts Recipes

Brownie Muffins

Servings: 10
Cooking Time: 15 Minutes
Ingredients:
- 2 eggs
- 96g all-purpose flour
- 1 tsp vanilla
- 130g powdered sugar
- 25g cocoa powder
- 37g pecans, chopped
- 1 tsp cinnamon
- 113g butter, melted

Directions:
1. In a bowl, whisk eggs, vanilla, butter, sugar, and cinnamon until well mixed.
2. Add cocoa powder and flour and stir until well combined.
3. Add pecans and fold well.
4. Pour batter into the silicone muffin moulds.
5. Insert a crisper plate in Ninja Foodi air fryer baskets.
6. Place muffin moulds in both baskets.
7. Select zone 1, then select “bake” mode and set the temperature to 360 degrees F for 15 minutes. Press “match” and then“start/stop” to begin.

Nutrition Info:
- (Per serving) Calories 210 | Fat 10.5g |Sodium 78mg | Carbs 28.7g | Fiber 1g | Sugar 20.2g | Protein 2.6g

Lava Cake

Servings: 4
Cooking Time: 10 Minutes
Ingredients:
- 1 cup semi-sweet chocolate chips
- 8 tablespoons butter
- 4 eggs
- 2 teaspoons vanilla extract
- ½ teaspoon salt
- 6 tablespoons all-purpose flour
-
- 1 cup powdered sugar
- For the chocolate filling:
- 2 tablespoons Nutella
- 1 tablespoon butter, softened
- 1 tablespoon powdered sugar

Directions:
1. Heat the chocolate chips and butter in a medium-sized microwave-safe bowl in 30-second intervals until thoroughly melted and smooth, stirring after each interval.
2. Whisk together the eggs, vanilla, salt, flour, and powdered sugar in a mixing bowl.
3. Combine the Nutella, softened butter, and powdered sugar in a separate bowl.
4. Spray 4 ramekins with oil and fill them halfway with the chocolate chip mixture. Fill each ramekin halfway with Nutella, then top with the remaining chocolate chip mixture, making sure the Nutella is well covered.
5. Install a crisper plate in both drawers. Place 2 ramekins in each drawer and insert the drawers into the unit.
6. Select zone 1, select AIR FRY, set temperature to 390 degrees F/ 200 degrees C, and set time to 22 minutes. Select MATCH to match zone 2 settings to zone 1. Press the START/STOP button to begin cooking.
7. Serve hot.

Nutrition Info:
- (Per serving) Calories 338 | Fat 21.2g | Sodium 1503mg | Carbs 5.1g | Fiber 0.3g | Sugar 4.6g | Protein 29.3g

Cinnamon Bread Twists

Servings: 4
Cooking Time: 15 Minutes

Ingredients:

- Bread Twists Dough
- 120g all-purpose flour
- 1 teaspoon baking powder
- ¼ teaspoon salt
- 150g fat free Greek yogurt
- Brushing
- 2 tablespoons light butter
- 2 tablespoons granulated sugar
- 1-2 teaspoons ground cinnamon, to taste

Directions:

1. Mix flour, salt and baking powder in a bowl.
2. Stir in yogurt and the rest of the dough ingredients in a bowl.
3. Mix well and make 8 inches long strips out of this dough.
4. Twist the strips and place them in the air fryer baskets.
5. Return the air fryer basket 1 to Zone 1, and basket 2 to Zone 2 of the Ninja Foodi 2-Basket Air Fryer.
6. Choose the "Air Fry" mode for Zone 1 at 375 degrees F and 15 minutes of cooking time.
7. Select the "MATCH COOK" option to copy the settings for Zone 2.
8. Initiate cooking by pressing the START/PAUSE BUTTON.
9. Flip the twists once cooked halfway through.
10. Mix butter with cinnamon and sugar in a bowl.
11. Brush this mixture over the twists.
12. Serve.

Nutrition Info:

- (Per serving) Calories 391 | Fat 24g |Sodium 142mg | Carbs 38.5g | Fiber 3.5g | Sugar 21g | Protein 6.6g

Honey Lime Pineapple

Servings: 4
Cooking Time: 10 Minutes

Ingredients:

- 562g pineapple chunks
- 55g brown sugar
- 30ml lime juice
- 63g honey

Directions:

1. In a bowl, mix pineapple, honey, lime juice, and brown sugar. Cover and place in refrigerator for 1 hour.
2. Insert a crisper plate in Ninja Foodi air fryer baskets.
3. Remove pineapple chunks from the marinade and place in both baskets.
4. Select zone 1 then select "air fry" mode and set the temperature to 390 degrees F for 10 minutes. Press "match" to match zone 2 settings to zone 1. Press "start/stop" to begin. Stir halfway through.

Nutrition Info:

- (Per serving) Calories 153 | Fat 0.2g |Sodium 5mg | Carbs 40.5g | Fiber 2g | Sugar 35.7g | Protein 0.8g

Cake In The Air Fryer

Servings:2
Cooking Time:30

Ingredients:

- 90 grams all-purpose flour
- Pinch of salt
- 1/2 teaspoon of baking powder
- ½ cup of tutti fruitti mix
- 2 eggs
- 1 teaspoon of vanilla extract
- 10 tablespoons of white sugar

Directions:

1. Take a bowl and add all-purpose flour, salt, and baking powder.
2. Stir it in a large bowl.
3. Whisk two eggs in a separate bowl and add vanilla extract, sugar and blend it with a hand beater.
4. Now combine wet ingredients with the dry ones.
5. Mix it well and pour it between two round pan that fits inside baskets.
6. Place the pans in both the baskets.
7. Now set the zone 1 basket to BAKE function at 310 for 30 minutes.
8. Select MATCH for zone two baskets.
9. Once it's done, serve and enjoy.

Nutrition Info:

- (Per serving) Calories 711| Fat4.8g| Sodium 143mg | Carbs 161g | Fiber 1.3g | Sugar 105g | Protein 10.2g

Bread Pudding

Servings: 4
Cooking Time: 15 Minutes

Ingredients:

- 2 cups bread cubes
- 1 egg
- ⅔ cup heavy cream
- ½ teaspoon vanilla extract
- ¼ cup sugar
- ¼ cup chocolate chips

Directions:

1. Grease two 4 inches baking dish with a cooking spray.
2. Divide the bread cubes in the baking dishes and sprinkle chocolate chips on top.
3. Beat egg with cream, sugar and vanilla in a bowl.
4. Divide this mixture in the baking dishes.
5. Place one pan in each air fryer basket.
6. Return the air fryer basket 1 to Zone 1, and basket 2 to Zone 2 of the Ninja Foodi 2-Basket Air Fryer.
7. Choose the "Air Fry" mode for Zone 1 at 350 degrees F and 15 minutes of cooking time.
8. Select the "MATCH COOK" option to copy the settings for Zone 2.
9. Initiate cooking by pressing the START/PAUSE BUTTON.
10. Allow the pudding to cool and serve.

Nutrition Info:

- (Per serving) Calories 149 | Fat 1.2g |Sodium 3mg | Carbs 37.6g | Fiber 5.8g | Sugar 29g | Protein 1.1g

Air Fryer Sweet Twists

Servings:2
Cooking Time:9
Ingredients:

- 1 box store-bought puff pastry
- ½ teaspoon cinnamon
- ½ teaspoon sugar
- ½ teaspoon black sesame seeds
- Salt, pinch
- 2 tablespoons Parmesan cheese, freshly grated

Directions:

1. Place the dough on a work surface.
2. Take a small bowl and mix cheese, sugar, salt, sesame seeds, and cinnamon.
3. Press this mixture on both sides of the dough.
4. Now, cut the pastry into 1" x 3" strips.
5. Twist each of the strips 2 times and then lay it onto the flat.
6. Transfer to both the air fryer baskets.
7. Select zone 1 to air fry mode at 400 degrees F for 9-10 minutes.
8. Select the MATCH button for the zone 2 basket.
9. Once cooked, serve.

Nutrition Info:

- (Per serving) Calories 140| Fat9.4g| Sodium 142mg | Carbs 12.3g | Fiber0.8 g | Sugar 1.2g | Protein 2g

Delicious Apple Fritters

Servings: 10
Cooking Time: 8 Minutes
Ingredients:

- 236g Bisquick
- 2 apples, peel & dice
- 158ml milk
- 30ml butter, melted
- 1 tsp cinnamon
- 24g sugar

Directions:

1. In a bowl, mix Bisquick, cinnamon, and sugar.
2. Add milk and mix until dough forms. Add apple and stir well.
3. Insert a crisper plate in Ninja Foodi air fryer baskets.
4. Make fritters from the mixture and place in both baskets. Brush fritters with melted butter.
5. Select zone 1 then select "air fry" mode and set the temperature to 360 degrees F for 10 minutes. Press "match" to match zone 2 settings to zone 1. Press "start/stop" to begin.

Nutrition Info:

- (Per serving) Calories 171 | Fat 6.7g |Sodium 352mg | Carbs 25.8g | Fiber 1.7g | Sugar 10.8g | Protein 2.7g

Air Fried Beignets

Servings: 6
Cooking Time: 17 Minutes.

Ingredients:

- Cooking spray
- ¼ cup white sugar
- ⅛ cup water
- ½ cup all-purpose flour
- 1 large egg, separated
- 1 ½ teaspoons butter, melted
- ½ teaspoon baking powder
- ½ teaspoon vanilla extract
- 1 pinch salt
- 2 tablespoons confectioners' sugar, or to taste

Directions:

1. Beat flour with water, sugar, egg yolk, baking powder, butter, vanilla extract, and salt in a large bowl until lumps-free.
2. Beat egg whites in a separate bowl and beat using an electric hand mixer until it forms soft peaks.
3. Add the egg white to the flour batter and mix gently until fully incorporated.
4. Divide the dough into small beignets and place them in the crisper plate.
5. Return the crisper plate to the Ninja Foodi Dual Zone Air Fryer.
6. Choose the Air Fry mode for Zone 1 and set the temperature to 390 degrees F and the time to 17 minutes.
7. Select the "MATCH" button to copy the settings for Zone 2.
8. Initiate cooking by pressing the START/STOP button.
9. And cook for another 4 minutes. Dust the cooked beignets with sugar.
10. Serve.

Nutrition Info:

- (Per serving) Calories 327 | Fat 14.2g |Sodium 672mg | Carbs 47.2g | Fiber 1.7g | Sugar 24.8g | Protein 4.4g

Apple Crisp

Servings: 8
Cooking Time: 14 Minutes.

Ingredients:

- 3 cups apples, chopped
- 1 tablespoon pure maple syrup
- 2 teaspoons lemon juice
- 3 tablespoons all-purpose flour
-
- ⅓ cup quick oats
- ¼ cup brown sugar
- 2 tablespoons light butter, melted
- ½ teaspoon cinnamon

Directions:

1. Toss the chopped apples with 1 tablespoon of all-purpose flour, cinnamon, maple syrup, and lemon juice in a suitable bowl.
2. Divide the apples in the two air fryer baskets with their crisper plates.
3. Whisk oats, brown sugar, and remaining all-purpose flour in a small bowl.
4. Stir in melted butter, then divide this mixture over the apples.
5. Return the crisper plate to the Ninja Foodi Dual Zone Air Fryer.
6. Select the Bake mode for Zone 1 and set the temperature to 375 degrees F and the time to 14 minutes.
7. Select the "MATCH" button to copy the settings for Zone 2.
8. Initiate cooking by pressing the START/STOP button.
9. Enjoy fresh.

Nutrition Info:

- (Per serving) Calories 258 | Fat 12.4g |Sodium 79mg | Carbs 34.3g | Fiber 1g | Sugar 17g | Protein 3.2g

Lemony Sweet Twists

Servings:2
Cooking Time:9

Ingredients:

- 1 box store-bought puff pastry
- ½ teaspoon lemon zest
- 1 tablespoon of lemon juice
- 2 teaspoons brown sugar
- Salt, pinch
- 2 tablespoons Parmesan cheese, freshly grated

Directions:

1. Put the puff pastry dough on a clean work area.
2. In a bowl, combine Parmesan cheese, brown sugar, salt, lemon zest, and lemon juice.
3. Press this mixture on both sides of the dough.
4. Now, cut the pastry into 1" x 4" strips.
5. Twist each of the strips.
6. Transfer to both the air fryer baskets.
7. Select zone 1 to air fry mode at 400 degrees F for 9-10 minutes.
8. Select match for zone 2 basket.
9. Once cooked, serve and enjoy.

Nutrition Info:

- (Per serving) Calories 156| Fat10g| Sodium 215mg | Carbs 14g | Fiber 0.4g | Sugar3.3 g | Protein 2.8g

Baked Apples

Servings: 4
Cooking Time: 15 Minutes

Ingredients:

- 4 apples
- 6 teaspoons raisins
- 2 teaspoons chopped walnuts
- 2 teaspoons honey
- ½ teaspoon cinnamon

Directions:

1. Chop off the head of the apples and scoop out the flesh from the center.
2. Stuff the apples with raisins, walnuts, honey and cinnamon.
3. Place these apples in the air fryer basket 1.
4. Return the air fryer basket 1 to Zone 1 of the Ninja Foodi 2-Basket Air Fryer.
5. Choose the "Air Fry" mode for Zone 1 and set the temperature to 350 degrees F and 15 minutes of cooking time.
6. Initiate cooking by pressing the START/PAUSE BUTTON.
7. Serve.

Nutrition Info:

- (Per serving) Calories 175 | Fat 13.1g |Sodium 154mg | Carbs 14g | Fiber 0.8g | Sugar 8.9g | Protein 0.7g

Cinnamon Sugar Dessert Fries

Servings: 4
Cooking Time: 15 Minutes
Ingredients:

- 2 sweet potatoes
- 1 tablespoon butter, melted
- 1 teaspoon butter, melted
- 2 tablespoons sugar
- ½ teaspoon ground cinnamon

Directions:

1. Peel and cut the sweet potatoes into skinny fries.
2. Coat the fries with 1 tablespoon of butter.
3. Install a crisper plate into each drawer. Place half the sweet potatoes in the zone 1 drawer and half in zone 2's, then insert the drawers into the unit.
4. Select zone 1, select AIR FRY, set temperature to 390 degrees F/ 200 degrees C, and set time to 15 minutes. Select MATCH to match zone 2 settings to zone 1. Press the START/STOP button to begin cooking.
5. When the time reaches 11 minutes, press START/STOP to pause the unit. Remove the drawers and flip the fries. Re-insert the drawers into the unit and press START/STOP to resume cooking.
6. Meanwhile, mix the 1 teaspoon of butter, the sugar, and the cinnamon in a large bowl.
7. When the fries are done, add them to the bowl, and toss them to coat.
8. Serve and enjoy!

Nutrition Info:

- (Per serving) Calories 110 | Fat 4g | Sodium 51mg | Carbs 18g | Fiber 2g | Sugar 10g | Protein 1g

Chocó Lava Cake

Servings: 4
Cooking Time: 10 Minutes
Ingredients:

- 3 eggs
- 3 egg yolks
- 70g dark chocolate, chopped
- 168g cups powdered sugar
- 96g all-purpose flour
- 1 tsp vanilla
- 113g butter
- ½ tsp salt

Directions:

1. Add chocolate and butter to a bowl and microwave for 30 seconds. Remove from oven and stir until smooth.
2. Add eggs, egg yolks, sugar, flour, vanilla, and salt into the melted chocolate and stir until well combined.
3. Pour batter into the four greased ramekins.
4. Insert a crisper plate in Ninja Foodi air fryer baskets.
5. Place ramekins in both baskets.
6. Select zone 1 then select "air fry" mode and set the temperature to 390 degrees F for 10 minutes. Press "match" to match zone 2 settings to zone 1. Press "start/stop" to begin.

Nutrition Info:

- (Per serving) Calories 687 | Fat 37.3g |Sodium 527mg | Carbs 78.3g | Fiber 1.5g | Sugar 57.4g | Protein 10.7g

Walnut Baklava Bites Pistachio Baklava Bites

Servings:12
Cooking Time: 10 Minutes

Ingredients:

- FOR THE WALNUT BAKLAVA BITES
- ¼ cup finely chopped walnuts
- 2 teaspoons cold unsalted butter, grated
- 2 teaspoons granulated sugar
- ½ teaspoon ground cinnamon
- 6 frozen phyllo shells (from a 1.9-ounce package), thawed
- FOR THE PISTACHIO BAKLAVA BITES
- ¼ cup finely chopped pistachios
-
- 2 teaspoons very cold unsalted butter, grated
- 2 teaspoons granulated sugar
- ¼ teaspoon ground cardamom (optional)
- 6 frozen phyllo shells (from a 1.9-ounce package), thawed
- FOR THE HONEY SYRUP
- ¼ cup hot water
- ¼ cup honey
- 2 teaspoons fresh lemon juice

Directions:

1. To prep the walnut baklava bites: In a small bowl, combine the walnuts, butter, sugar, and cinnamon. Spoon the filling into the phyllo shells.
2. To prep the pistachio baklava bites: In a small bowl, combine the pistachios, butter, sugar, and cardamom (if using). Spoon the filling into the phyllo shells.
3. To cook the baklava bites: Install a crisper plate in each of the two baskets. Place the walnut baklava bites in the Zone 1 basket and insert the basket in the unit. Place the pistachio baklava bites in the Zone 2 basket and insert the basket in the unit.
4. Select Zone 1, select BAKE, set the temperature to 330°F, and set the timer to 10 minutes. Press MATCH COOK to match Zone 2 settings to Zone 1.
5. Press START/PAUSE to begin cooking.
6. When cooking is complete, the shells will be golden brown and crisp.
7. To make the honey syrup: In a small bowl, whisk together the hot water, honey, and lemon juice. Dividing evenly, pour the syrup over the baklava bites (you may hear a crackling sound).
8. Let cool completely before serving, about 1 hour.

Nutrition Info:

- (Per serving) Calories: 262; Total fat: 16g; Saturated fat: 3g; Carbohydrates: 29g; Fiber: 1g; Protein: 2g; Sodium: 39mg

Strawberry Shortcake

Servings: 8
Cooking Time: 9 Minutes

Ingredients:

- Strawberry topping
- 1-pint strawberries sliced
- ½ cup confectioner's sugar substitute
- Shortcake
- 2 cups Carbquick baking biscuit mix
- ¼ cup butter cold, cubed
- ½ cup confectioner's sugar substitute
- Pinch salt
- ⅔ cup water
- Garnish: sugar free whipped cream

Directions:

1. Mix the shortcake ingredients in a bowl until smooth.
2.
3. Divide the dough into 6 biscuits.
4. Place the biscuits in the air fryer basket 1.
5. Return the air fryer basket 1 to Zone 1 of the Ninja Foodi 2-Basket Air Fryer.
6. Choose the "Air Fry" mode for Zone 1 and set the temperature 400 degrees F and 9 minutes of cooking time.
7. Initiate cooking by pressing the START/PAUSE BUTTON.
8. Mix strawberries with sugar in a saucepan and cook until the mixture thickens.
9. Slice the biscuits in half and add strawberry sauce in between two halves of a biscuit.
10. Serve.

Nutrition Info:

- (Per serving) Calories 157 | Fat 1.3g |Sodium 27mg | Carbs 1.3g | Fiber 1g | Sugar 2.2g | Protein 8.2g

Chocolate Cookies

Servings: 18
Cooking Time: 7 Minutes

Ingredients:

- 96g flour
- 57g butter, softened
- 15ml milk
- 7.5g cocoa powder
- 80g chocolate chips
- ½ tsp vanilla
- 35g sugar
- ¼ tsp baking soda
- Pinch of salt

Directions:

1. In a bowl, mix flour, cocoa powder, sugar, baking soda, vanilla, butter, milk, and salt until well combined.
2. Add chocolate chips and mix well.
3. Insert a crisper plate in Ninja Foodi air fryer baskets.
4. Make cookies from the mixture and place in both baskets.
5. Select zone 1 then select "air fry" mode and set the temperature to 360 degrees F for 7 minutes. Press "match" to match zone 2 settings to zone 1. Press "start/stop" to begin.

Nutrition Info:

- (Per serving) Calories 82 | Fat 4.1g |Sodium 47mg | Carbs 10.7g | Fiber 0.4g | Sugar 6.2g | Protein 1g

Jelly Donuts

Servings: 4
Cooking Time: 5 Minutes

Ingredients:

- 1 package Pillsbury Grands (Homestyle)
- ½ cup seedless raspberry jelly
- 1 tablespoon butter, melted
- ½ cup sugar

Directions:

1. Install a crisper plate in both drawers. Place half of the biscuits in the zone 1 drawer and half in zone 2's, then insert the drawers into the unit. You may need to cook in batches.
2. Select zone 1, select AIR FRY, set temperature to 390 degrees F/ 200 degrees C, and set time to 22 minutes. Select MATCH to match zone 2 settings to zone 1. Press the START/STOP button to begin cooking.
3. Place the sugar into a wide bowl with a flat bottom.
4. Baste all sides of the cooked biscuits with the melted butter and roll in the sugar to cover completely.
5. Using a long cake tip, pipe 1–2 tablespoons of raspberry jelly into each biscuit. You've now got raspberry-filled donuts!

Nutrition Info:

- (Per serving) Calories 252 | Fat 7g | Sodium 503mg | Carbs 45g | Fiber 0g | Sugar 23g | Protein 3g

Chocolate Chip Muffins

Servings:2
Cooking Time:15
Ingredients:

- Salt, pinch
- 2 eggs
- 1/3 cup brown sugar
- 1/3 cup butter
- 4 tablespoons of milk
-
- ¼ teaspoon of vanilla extract
- ½ teaspoon of baking powder
- 1 cup all-purpose flour
- 1 pouch chocolate chips, 35 grams

Directions:

1. Take 4 oven-safe ramekins that are the size of a cup and layer them with muffin papers.
2. In a bowl, whisk the egg, brown sugar, butter, milk, and vanilla extract.
3. Whisk it all very well with an electric hand beater.
4. Now, in a second bowl, mix the flour, baking powder, and salt.
5. Now, mix the dry ingredients slowly into the wet ingredients.
6. Now, at the end fold in the chocolate chips and mix them well
7. Divide this batter into 4 ramekins.
8. Now, divide it between both zones.
9. Set the time for zone 1 to 15 minutes at 350 degrees F, at AIRFRY mode.
10. Select the MATCH button for the zone 2 basket.
11. Check if not done, and let it AIR FRY for one more minute.
12. Once it is done, serve.

Nutrition Info:

- (Per serving) Calories 757| Fat40.3g| Sodium 426mg | Carbs 85.4g | Fiber 2.2g | Sugar 30.4g | Protein 14.4g

Air Fried Bananas

Servings: 4
Cooking Time: 13 Minutes.
Ingredients:

- 4 bananas, sliced
- 1 avocado oil cooking spray

Directions:

1. Spread the banana slices in the two crisper plates in a single layer.
2. Drizzle avocado oil over the banana slices.
3. Return the crisper plate to the Ninja Foodi Dual Zone Air Fryer.
4. Choose the Air Fry mode for Zone 1 and set the temperature to 350 degrees F and the time to 13 minutes.
5. Select the "MATCH" button to copy the settings for Zone 2.
6. Initiate cooking by pressing the START/STOP button.
7. Serve.

Nutrition Info:

- (Per serving) Calories 149 | Fat 1.2g |Sodium 3mg | Carbs 37.6g | Fiber 5.8g | Sugar 29g | Protein 1.1g

Cinnamon-sugar "churros" With Caramel Sauce

Servings:4
Cooking Time: 10 Minutes
Ingredients:

- FOR THE "CHURROS"
- 1 sheet frozen puff pastry, thawed
- Butter-flavored cooking spray
- 1 tablespoon granulated sugar
- 1 teaspoon ground cinnamon
- FOR THE CARAMEL SAUCE
-
- ½ cup packed light brown sugar
- 2 tablespoons unsalted butter, cut into small pieces
- ¼ cup heavy (whipping) cream
- 2 teaspoons vanilla extract
- ⅛ teaspoon kosher salt

Directions:

1. To prep the "churros": Cut the puff pastry crosswise into 4 rectangles. Fold each piece in half lengthwise to make a long thin "churro."
2. To prep the caramel sauce: Measure the brown sugar, butter, cream, and vanilla into an ovenproof ramekin or bowl (no need to stir).
3. To cook the "churros" and caramel sauce: Install a crisper plate in the Zone 1 basket. Place the "churros" in the basket and insert the basket in the unit. Place the ramekin in the Zone 2 basket and insert the basket in the unit.
4. Select Zone 1, select AIR FRY, set the temperature to 330°F, and set the timer to 10 minutes.
5. Select Zone 2, select BAKE, set the temperature to 350°F, and set the timer to 10 minutes. Select SMART FINISH.
6. Press START/PAUSE to begin cooking.
7. When the Zone 2 timer reads 5 minutes, press START/PAUSE. Remove the basket and stir the caramel. Reinsert the basket and press START/PAUSE to resume cooking.
8. When cooking is complete, the "churros" will be golden brown and cooked through and the caramel sauce smooth.
9. Spritz each "churro" with cooking spray and sprinkle generously with the granulated sugar and cinnamon.
10. Stir the salt into the caramel sauce. Let cool for 5 to 10 minutes before serving. Note that the caramel will thicken as it cools.

Nutrition Info:

- (Per serving) Calories: 460; Total fat: 26g; Saturated fat: 14g; Carbohydrates: 60g; Fiber: 1.5g; Protein: 5g; Sodium: 254mg

Moist Chocolate Espresso Muffins

Servings: 8
Cooking Time: 18 Minutes
Ingredients:

- 1 egg
- 177ml milk
- ½ tsp baking soda
- ½ tsp espresso powder
- ½ tsp baking powder
- 50g cocoa powder
-
- 78ml vegetable oil
- 1 tsp apple cider vinegar
- 1 tsp vanilla
- 150g brown sugar
- 150g all-purpose flour
- ½ tsp salt

Directions:

1. In a bowl, whisk egg, vinegar, oil, brown sugar, vanilla, and milk.
2. Add flour, cocoa powder, baking soda, baking powder, espresso powder, and salt and stir until well combined.
3. Pour batter into the silicone muffin moulds.
4. Insert a crisper plate in Ninja Foodi air fryer baskets.
5. Place muffin moulds in both baskets.
6. Select zone 1 then select "bake" mode and set the temperature to 320 degrees F for 18 minutes. Press match cook to match zone 2 settings to zone 1. Press "start/stop" to begin.

Nutrition Info:

- (Per serving) Calories 222 | Fat 11g |Sodium 251mg | Carbs 29.6g | Fiber 2g | Sugar 14.5g | Protein 4g

Strawberry Nutella Hand Pies

Servings: 8
Cooking Time: 10 Minutes

Ingredients:

- 1 tube pie crust dough
- 3–4 strawberries, finely chopped
- Nutella
- Sugar
- Coconut oil cooking spray

Directions:

1. Roll out the pie dough and place it on a baking sheet. Cut out hearts using a 3-inch heart-shaped cookie cutter as precisely as possible.
2. Gather the leftover dough into a ball and roll it out thinly to make a few more heart shapes. For 8 hand pies, I was able to get 16 hearts from one tube of pie crust.
3. Set aside a baking tray lined with parchment paper.
4. Spread a dollop of Nutella (approximately 1 teaspoon) on one of the hearts. Add a few strawberry pieces to the mix. Add a pinch of sugar to the top.
5. Place another heart on top and use a fork to tightly crimp the edges. Gently poke holes in the top of the pie with a fork. Place on a baking sheet. Repeat for all the pies.
6. All of the pies on the tray should be sprayed with coconut oil.
7. Install a crisper plate in both drawers. Place half the pies in the zone 1 drawer and half in zone 2's, then insert the drawers into the unit.
8. Select zone 1, select BAKE, set temperature to 390 degrees F/ 200 degrees C, and set time to 10 minutes. Select MATCH to match zone 2 settings to zone 1. Press the START/STOP button to begin cooking.

Nutrition Info:

- (Per serving) Calories 41 | Fat 2.1g | Sodium 18mg | Carbs 5.5g | Fiber 0.4g | Sugar 4.1g | Protein 0.4g

Chocolate Pudding

Servings: 2
Cooking Time: 12 Minutes

Ingredients:

- 1 egg
- 32g all-purpose flour
- 35g cocoa powder
- 50g sugar
- 57g butter, melted
- ½ tsp baking powder

Directions:

1. In a bowl, mix flour, cocoa powder, sugar, and baking powder.
2. Add egg and butter and stir until well combined.
3. Pour batter into the two greased ramekins.
4. Insert a crisper plate in Ninja Foodi air fryer baskets.
5. Place ramekins in both baskets.
6. Select zone 1 then select "bake" mode and set the temperature to 375 degrees F for 12 minutes. Press match cook to match zone 2 settings to zone 1. Press "start/stop" to begin.

Nutrition Info:

- (Per serving) Calories 512 | Fat 27.3g |Sodium 198mg | Carbs 70.6g | Fiber 4.7g | Sugar 50.5g | Protein 7.2g

Fried Dough With Roasted Strawberries

Servings:4

Cooking Time: 20 Minutes

Ingredients:

- FOR THE FRIED DOUGH
- 6 ounces refrigerated pizza dough, at room temperature
- 2 tablespoons all-purpose flour, for dusting
- 4 tablespoons vegetable oil
- 2 tablespoons powdered sugar
- FOR THE ROASTED STRAWBERRIES
- 2 cups frozen whole strawberries
- 2 tablespoons granulated sugar

Directions:

1. To prep the fried dough: Divide the dough into four equal portions.
2. Dust a clean work surface with the flour. Place one dough portion on the surface and use a rolling pin to roll to a ⅛-inch thickness. Rub both sides of the dough with 1 tablespoon of oil. Repeat with remaining dough portions and oil.
3. To prep the strawberries: Place the strawberries in the Zone 2 basket. Sprinkle the granulated sugar on top.
4. To cook the fried dough and strawberries: Install a crisper plate in the Zone 1 basket. Place 2 dough portions in the basket and insert the basket in the unit. Insert the Zone 2 basket in the unit.
5. Select Zone 1, select AIR FRY, set the temperature to 400°F, and set the timer to 18 minutes.
6. Select Zone 2, select ROAST, set the temperature to 330°F, and set the timer to 20 minutes. Select SMART FINISH.
7. Press START/PAUSE to begin cooking.
8. When both timers read 8 minutes, press START/PAUSE. Remove the Zone 1 basket and transfer the fried dough to a cutting board. Place the 2 remaining dough portions in the basket, then reinsert the basket. Remove the Zone 2 basket and stir the strawberries. Reinsert the basket and press START/PAUSE to resume cooking.
9. When cooking is complete, the dough should be cooked through and the strawberries soft and jammy.
10. Sprinkle the fried dough with powdered sugar. Gently mash the strawberries with a fork. Spoon the strawberries onto each fried dough portion and serve.

Nutrition Info:

- (Per serving) Calories: 304; Total fat: 15g; Saturated fat: 2.5g; Carbohydrates: 38g; Fiber: 0.5g; Protein: 3g; Sodium: 421mg

INDEX

A

Acorn Squash Slices 91
Air Fried Bananas 107
Air Fried Beignets 102
Air Fried Chicken Legs 55
Air Fried Lamb Chops 50
Air Fried Okra 97
Air Fryer Calamari 81
Air Fryer Meatloaves 52
Air Fryer Sausage Patties 17
Air Fryer Sweet Twists 101
Air Fryer Vegetables 92
Air-fried Turkey Breast With Roasted Green Bean Casserole 63
Apple Crisp 102

B

Bacon And Egg Omelet 19
Bagels 14
Baked Apples 103
Balsamic Duck Breast 65
Balsamic Steak Tips With Roasted Asparagus And Mushroom Medley 43
Balsamic Vegetables 92
Balsamic-glazed Tofu With Roasted Butternut Squash 94
Banana Muffins 17
Bang Bang Shrimp 78
Bang-bang Chicken 60
Barbecue Ribs With Roasted Green Beans And Shallots 45
Bbq Corn 93
Beef & Broccoli 46
Beef And Bean Taquitos With Mexican Rice 41
Beef Jerky Pineapple Jerky 30
Beets With Orange Gremolata And Goat's Cheese 86
Blackened Mahimahi With Honey-roasted Carrots 69
Blueberry Coffee Cake And Maple Sausage Patties 15
Brazilian Chicken Drumsticks 62
Bread Pudding 100
Breakfast Cheese Sandwich 23
Breakfast Stuffed Peppers 20
Brownie Muffins 98
Brussels Sprouts 95
Buffalo Seitan With Crispy Zucchini Noodles 87
Buffalo Wings Honey-garlic Wings 34
Buttermilk Biscuits With Roasted Stone Fruit Compote 12
Buttermilk Fried Chicken 62

C

Cake In The Air Fryer 100
Caprese Panini With Zucchini Chips 96
Cheese Corn Fritters 29
Cheese Stuffed Mushrooms 25
Cheesy Potatoes With Asparagus 85
Chicken & Veggies 58
Chicken And Potatoes 56
Chicken Caprese 56
Chicken Crescent Wraps 33
Chicken Drumettes 54
Chicken Drumsticks 58
Chicken Fajitas With Street Corn 67
Chicken Kebabs 60
Chicken Parmesan 66
Chicken Parmesan With Roasted Lemon-parmesan Broccoli 53
Chicken Stuffed Mushrooms 33
Chili Chicken Wings 66
Chili-lime Crispy Chickpeas Pizza-seasoned Crispy Chickpeas 31
Chipotle Beef 52
Chocó Lava Cake 104
Chocolate Chip Muffins 107
Chocolate Cookies 106
Chocolate Pudding 109
Cinnamon Bread Twists 99
Cinnamon Sugar Dessert Fries 104
Cinnamon-sugar "churros" With Caramel Sauce 108
Coconut Chicken Tenders With Broiled Utica Greens 57
Cornish Hen 54
Cornish Hen With Asparagus 64
Crab Cake Poppers 28
Crispy Chickpeas 25
Crispy Popcorn Shrimp 29
Crispy Sesame Chicken 55
Curly Fries 82

D

Delicious Apple Fritters 101
Delicious Potatoes & Carrots 82

E

Easy Pancake Doughnuts 16
Egg White Muffins 16
Egg With Baby Spinach 13

F

Fish And Chips 80
Flavourful Mexican Cauliflower 95
Fried Avocado Tacos 88
Fried Dough With Roasted Strawberries 110
Fried Olives 94
Fried Pickles 28
Furikake Salmon 74

G

Garlic Shrimp With Pasta Alfredo 72
Garlic-herb Fried Squash 84
Garlic-rosemary Pork Loin With Scalloped Potatoes And Cauliflower 47
Glazed Scallops 75
Gochujang Brisket 38
Greek Chicken Meatballs 59
Green Beans With Baked Potatoes 86

H

Hash Browns 13
Hasselback Potatoes 93
Healthy Chickpea Fritters 36
Healthy Lobster Cakes 77
Healthy Oatmeal Muffins 19
Healthy Spinach Balls 37
Herb Lemon Mussels 69
Herb Tuna Patties 72
Honey Banana Oatmeal 21
Honey Lime Pineapple 99

I

Italian Sausages With Peppers, Potatoes, And Onions 44

J

Jalapeño Popper Chicken 32
Jelly Donuts 106
Jerk Tofu With Roasted Cabbage 83
Jerk-rubbed Pork Loin With Carrots And Sage 44
Juicy Duck Breast 65
Juicy Pork Chops 51

L

Lamb Chops With Dijon Garlic 46
Lava Cake 98
Lemon Pepper Fish Fillets 75
Lemon-cream Cheese Danishes Cherry Danishes 20
Lemony Sweet Twists 103

M

Mac And Cheese Balls 35
Moist Chocolate Espresso Muffins 108
Mongolian Beef With Sweet Chili Brussels Sprouts 48

O

Onion Rings 32

P

Parmesan Crush Chicken 26
Pepper Egg Cups 18
Pork Chops And Potatoes 38
Pork Chops With Broccoli 42
Pork Katsu With Seasoned Rice 49
Potato Tater Tots 27
Pretzel-crusted Catfish 71
Pumpkin French Toast Casserole With Sweet And Spicy Twisted Bacon 11

Q

Quiche Breakfast Peppers 14
Quinoa Patties 89

R

Ravioli 30
Roasted Oranges 24
Roasted Salmon And Parmesan Asparagus 74
Rosemary Asparagus & Potatoes 84

S

Salmon Nuggets 71
Salmon With Green Beans 73
Sausage & Butternut Squash 23
Sausage Hash And Baked Eggs 24
Seafood Shrimp Omelet 80
Short Ribs & Root Vegetables 40
Shrimp Po'boys With Sweet Potato Fries 70
Shrimp Skewers 78
Shrimp With Lemon And Pepper 73
Smoked Salmon 79
Southwestern Fish Fillets 77
Spicy Chicken 59
Spicy Chicken Tenders 36
Spicy Salmon Fillets 81
Spinach And Red Pepper Egg Cups With Coffee-glazed Canadian Bacon 18
Spinach Egg Muffins 22
Steak And Asparagus Bundles 51
Steak And Mashed Creamy Potatoes 50
Steak Bites With Cowboy Butter 42
Steak Fajitas With Onions And Peppers 40
Strawberry Baked Oats Chocolate Peanut Butter Baked Oats 22
Strawberry Nutella Hand Pies 109
Strawberry Shortcake 105
Stuffed Mushrooms 35
Stuffed Sweet Potatoes 91
Sweet Bites 27
Sweet Potato Hash 21
Sweet Potatoes With Honey Butter 85
Sweet-and-sour Chicken With Pineapple Cauliflower Rice 61

T

Tasty Pork Skewers 43
Tasty Sweet Potato Wedges 37
Tater Tots 34
Tilapia With Mojo And Crispy Plantains 68
Tomahawk Steak 39
Tuna Patties 76
Two-way Salmon 79

V

Veggie Burgers With "fried" Onion Rings 90

W

Walnut Baklava Bites Pistachio Baklava Bites 105
Wings With Corn On The Cob 64

Y

Yogurt Lamb Chops 39

Z

Zucchini Chips 26

Printed in Great Britain
by Amazon

22970712R00064